FAITH to ACT

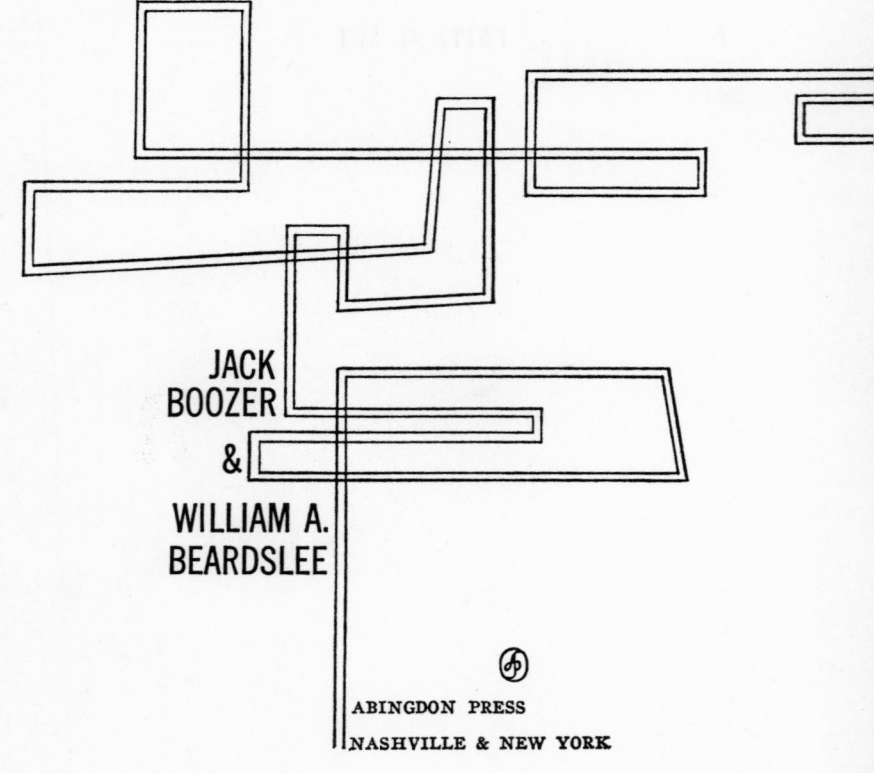

JACK
BOOZER

&

WILLIAM A.
BEARDSLEE

ABINGDON PRESS

NASHVILLE & NEW YORK

FAITH to ACT

*An Essay on the Meaning
of Christian Existence*

FAITH TO ACT

To Our Students

for whom we have tried to write
to whom we have tried to listen
with whom we have shared the search

PREFACE

In our time the crisis of faith and the crisis of action are deeply interwoven. This book searches for and speaks to the point of juncture between faith and action, seeking to explore the roots and resources of action in faith. It is not a book about the traditional problems of Christian ethics, but a study of how faith may and must move toward and into action.

Christian faith in our time is struggling to overcome a sizeable gap between the concrete and changing demands made on us by the actual situation we confront, and an overformalized code of accepted Christian behavior. We present an interpretation of the movement of faith toward action which embodies both a recognition of freedom and of the impossibility of legislating responsible decision in advance, and a recognition of the continuing presence of structures, of *formed* claims upon us, which give specific shape to acts of love.

Though we have each criticized each other's work, the principal responsibility for Chapters I, V, VII, and VIII lies with J. B., and that for Chapters II, III, IV, and VI with W. A. B.

Faith to Act

We are indebted to the Ossabaw Island Project for a time of joint work and discussion, and to the Emory University Research Committee for assistance. Numerous colleagues, friends, and students have read and criticized our work as it was in progress, and have helped us achieve a greater degree of clarity. We are especially indebted to Mr. C. Shelby Rooks for criticism of Chapters VI and VII. Mrs. Linda Kravitz, Miss Barbara Harkins, and Mrs. Kay Sims typed the manuscript in several versions. The index was prepared by Raymond P. Cowan.

JACK BOOZER

WILLIAM A. BEARDSLEE

CONTENTS

I
The Moral Dilemma of Contemporary Man

For I tell you, unless your righteousness exceeds that of the scribes and Pharisees, you will never enter the kingdom of heaven. (Matt. 5:20.)

But the tax collector, standing far off, would not even lift up his eyes to heaven, but beat his breast, saying, "God, be merciful to me a sinner!" (Luke 18:13.)

Two statements have been made recently which stand in strange juxtaposition. The first is from the mother of a college student who is quite worried that her son will face such attack, ridicule, and criticism in college that he will abandon the Christian faith of his earlier years.

Why can't we devise a method to enable college students to think through to a dynamic religion without destroying what little faith, spirituality, and knowledge they already possess? Is it not our

11

duty to nurture every bit of Christianity a person has, so that it might grow in his heart?

No one can give another person his beliefs or his religion. Each person must think for himself. But he needs help in order to think. Nobody's religion ever should be finished. I know the theory is to shock students into thinking things out for themselves, but we don't pull up a plant by the roots to make it grow more luxuriant. There is too great a chance it will die completely. Youths, on the whole, do not have the resources to handle freedom properly.

I am concerned about the fruit of the new teaching. It seems to be creating doubt and uncertainty about God and man. If it produced happiness, love, peace, faith, or good Christianity, it would be worth it. Instead, we have lawlessness, sexual immorality, lack of respect for parents or older people, doubt and fear. There is no worthwhile fruit.[1]

The second statement is from a student, a senior in college. He makes the statement early in his last year, reflecting on his intellectual and religious pilgrimage during the college years.

In a positive sense I was turning to a life of independent thought, of political responsibility for a more just social order, to the meaning of my own participation in the human drama, and to a new kind of care for people.

In a negative sense I was also turning away from some things. I had come to identify the church with a negative ethic, church politics, anti-Catholicism, and a lack of sensitivity to things more important than smoking, drinking, dancing, and tithing.

One wonders whether these two persons are living in the same culture at the same time, yet one knows very well how entirely possible it is that these two persons are not only

[1] Reprinted from *Together*, Vol. IX, No. 11, November 1965, p. 46.

contemporaries, but that they could actually be mother and son. What the mother accepts as her vocation to transmit to the next generation, the student feels he must reject in order to be honest and responsible in his own life. There is, of course, the gap between the generations which affects the situation, but the issue between parent and student is more substantial than that. There is a sharp difference between them as to the way they understand faith, morality, and education.

To the mother the Bible, the church, faith, and morality are woven together in one fabric and are encountered in a history and society which are thought to be stable. Indeed, the relation between faith and morality is so orderly that a person should be able to move through adolescence and college, from childhood to maturity, under Christian sponsorship without shock or trauma. To the student, on the other hand, the neat unity of faith and morality obscured the critical factor of his own feeling for the holy and the right, causing him to turn away from the church in order to maintain a moral integrity.

The mother and the student represent the kind of misunderstanding that characterizes many aspects of our lives. It would be too easy a solution to side altogether with one or the other. To do that would really be no solution to the problem. In order to avoid such an unfortunate "either/or," we must move back from the impasse and raise basic questions about the meaning of faith, morality, and the church. Surely no one would maintain that dishonesty is required of the Christian, but neither can one accept the mother's view of the relation between faith and morality as being the only one possible. She is right in seeing a relationship between faith and morality. She is wrong in the relationship she sees. The student is right about the more crucial ethical problems. He is wrong in assuming that Christian faith is not interested in these problems.

The fact that the issue could arise in this way suggests that the problem of an authentic morality is a continuing one for faith, and that more precise thought about the nature of Christian faith might well change our conception of how faith is related to morality, changing, as well, the answer to the educational question about how faith and morality are shared with others. The purpose of this entire book is to suggest a kind of "faith-action" which is characteristic of the Christian. Such a purpose will be within clearer view if we now elaborate the gap between the mother and the student as illustrative of the kind of perplexity any thoughtful person feels before the press of the moral question.

THE NATURE OF THE PROBLEM

Every significant problem man faces is confusingly complicated. It is all too easy for one to become sophisticated to the point of recognizing the maze which each problem presents and to fall either into paralysis or into an oversimplification of the issue. The tendency within the religious communities, unfortunately, is to oversimplify every moral problem. "If you just do the right thing, this problem will work out for you." How often we have heard that kind of counsel! Whatever truth there may be in the advice, the counsel is moot because we always ask a question within a situation in which neither we nor others have done the completely right thing. Perhaps the counsel typifies our ethical dilemma by implying that there is a simple "right thing" which one is able to know and to do. It is our contention that there is no specific "right thing" which all Christians should do in a particular issue, nor is a Christian necessarily stunned into inaction, but that he is called to act as a Christian man in a situation with an obligation to do *something* in spite of the fact that he is not able to do *everything.*

The error of conventional religious ethics is that it expresses the obligation of the Christian so specifically that faith is telescoped into ethics with the result that faith becomes dependent upon ethics. This turn of things not only flies in the face of Paul's emphasis on "grace alone," but it also encourages a community to emphasize the virtues which are easiest. In this situation it is quite possible for one to live under the illusion that he is Christian because he is honest or generous or abstinent or a "lover of peace." Morality then becomes moralistic and therefore sub-Christian. Against a moralistic identification of faith and ethics, we must insist, at the outset, that Christian morality is not simply the property of an action, a listing of right things to do, but the action of persons in faith.

Conventional Christian faith also becomes pietistic and therefore not Christian because a "good conscience" is claimed on the basis of the righteousness of man's action and not upon the basis of God's forgiveness. The moralist and the pietist distort Christian morality because they ask the wrong question upon the wrong premise and for the wrong reason.[2] A "sensitive conscience" as to what is right is more basic to Christian morality than is a "good conscience." Almost inevitably the

---

[2] The question is wrong because it asks how to please God, not how to serve the neighbor. The premise is wrong because it implies a definition of a Christian in terms of particular actions, without regard to intentions and motives. The motivation of the question is wrong because it rests upon the assumption that God's acceptance of us is contingent upon our doing the right thing.

"good conscience" is defined in terms which indicate status within a certain social and political orientation, a certain way of understanding things. If we catalog the virtues within a particular orientation, we run the great danger of being provincial and naïve; provincial in that we restrict the virtue to its meaning within a particular group, naïve in that we interpret the formative power of a virtue in terms of its specific application rather than understanding a specific instance of a virtue (justice, for instance) in relation to the formative basis of that virtue.

Loyalty is certainly one of the most significant virtues in human life. We teach one another in all sorts of groups the value of loyalty, loyalty to the team, to the family, to the club, to the product, to the church, to the nation. What do we do, however, in the presence of a conflict of loyalties? Should one continue to be loyal to a group which restricts or prejudices one's relation to other people? Should one continue to be loyal to the "gang" when the group is seen to be anti-social? Should one continue to be loyal to a nation when the policies of the nation become anti-human? Should one continue to be loyal to a church when the church reinforces differences between men in a prejudicial way?

In all these cases it is clear that a virtue defined provincially, as applicable only within a particular group, is highly questionable as a virtue. If justice is justice only to fellow Pennsylvanians or fellow Christians or fellow Aryans, the crucial question of justice in the more universal sense as being a property of humanness does not arise. The "just" Pennsylvanian, the "just" Christian, and the "just" Aryan may not be "just" *men* at all. If this is true, and if we define justice within the limited province of Pennsylvania or of Christianness, we become provincial and, as far as the human virtues are concerned, suspect.

It is the temptation of every group to define virtue quite explicitly in terms of the things which strengthen the group, assuming that anything which benefits the group is of benefit to the individual. "What is good for General Motors is good for the United States," says one. "What is good for the Methodist is good for all men," says another. Still another claims: "What is good for the United States is good for the world." To say that traditional Christianity places more importance upon the "good conscience" than upon the "sensitive conscience" is to point up the way a group, largely without intention, perverts the real meaning of moral virtue by defining a virtue completely in terms of a provincial orientation. Hence a person who grows up in a radically segregated society may well accept a "moral responsibility" to continue the pattern of segregation as essential to social stability. Another person will find himself thinking that any drinking of alcoholic beverages is wrong because the particular group in which he lives is so completely committed to total abstinence. The easy way in which some people identify temperance with total abstinence illustrates the point.

Varying the issue a little, another person will assume that all sexual relations are morally right within marriage because his group has taught so emphatically that sexual intercourse outside marriage is wrong. Thomas Merton has chided us for assuming that all our bombs are blessed by the angels because our enemy has been branded as evil, as God's enemy too. "It is one thing to trust in God because one depends upon Him in reality, and quite another to assume that he will bless our bombs because the Russians are atheists and He cannot possibly approve of them." [3]

Yet in pointing out the provincial error into which our particular communities fall, we do not intend to deny the importance of the particular communities. Stanley Kaufmann makes a comment about the work of D. H. Lawrence that illuminates this question. "That he is, in the most rigorous view, a great writer is worth doubting. That he is an important one is past question. The paradox of Lawrence, I believe, is that—unlike truly great artists—the more you have liberated yourself the less he means to you." [4] The test of the virtue of the particular community is the extent to which its virtues continue to be viable as one liberates himself from the limited dimensions of that community. If a community has neglected the sensitive conscience in favor of the good conscience it is highly likely that the virtues of that community are more "preferences" than virtues, and that the moral growth of the liberated person will require the rejection of the values of his native community. In any event it is clear that one aspect of the problem of Christian ethics is the provincial cast which is accidentally given to the entire moral question. The problem for the community is to find a way without provincialism to impart a concrete way of being and action. The problem for the individual is to discover a morality that will be viable for him as a man far beyond the province of a particular community. The distance between the positions of the parent and the student sketched above

[3] From the article "Conjectures of a Guilty Bystander," *Life,* August 5, 1966, p. 72, anticipatory of the publication of the book.
[4] In a review of *Lady Chatterley's Lover. The New Republic,* May 22, 1959, p. 16.

indicates the costliness of moral integrity in a situation of deep erosion on both sides.

The cultural Christianity of our day has also ended in being naïve about conscience and again emphasizing the good conscience at the expense of the sensitive conscience. Here the mistake is that of taking the fruit for the tree, in placing the whole weight of morality on the property of an action. It may well be that philosophical ethics is primarily concerned with the rightness of an action. Christian ethics, on the contrary, is just as concerned with intention or motive as with action, just as concerned with the context within which an action is committed as with the action itself. It would be interesting to speculate about whether there are any actions which, quite apart from motive and situation, are always wrong.[5] At the moment, the influence of intention and situation upon the "morality" of an action are presupposed. The question here is not whether it is right or wrong to make a profit, but under what conditions; not whether it is right or wrong to feel or express sexual desire, but under what conditions; not whether it is right or wrong to kill, but under what conditions; not whether it is right or wrong to drink or to segregate/integrate or to automate, but under what conditions.

Pandora's box is open, and in order to say that the morality of every action is dependent upon the intention and the

[5] We have put such a question to our students. At the outset they were quite sure that there were a number of actions which were always wrong, no matter what the circumstances might be. Under criticism, however, they gave ground and found it difficult to name any particular action in this category. They came close to listing brutality to children, racial segregation, idolatrous devotion to the state, and "holy war," but were really not sure that any action would in itself always be wrong.

situation as well as the action, we are exposed to all sorts of criticism accusing us of being relativistic and of failing to appreciate the "act" by implying that the intention makes it moral or immoral. To the charge that we are relativistic, we reply that we advocate a morality that is relative to every possible situation but "relativistic" in none. To the charge that we slight the importance of action we can only say that this is not our intention. We are thoroughly in accord with the statement attributed to Bonhoeffer: "Only he who cries out for the Jews has a right to sing Gregorian chants." [6]

The only thing that is always right for the Christian is to love. The only thing that is always wrong for the Christian is the failure to love. Everything else that he does depends upon the situation. Nothing one does without love is properly a Christian action, no matter how courageous, patriotic, loyal, and just it may appear to be. This would suggest that although there is a relation between good fruit and a sound tree, it would be a mistake to assert their identity and to begin to try to polish fruit rather than to spray and prune trees. In the realm of morality it would be extremely shortsighted to encourage people to imitate the good deeds of virtuous persons. Virtue is not transferable in that way. Virtue imitated for virtue's sake is not real virtue but rather a pale and insipid copy of the real thing. Virtue is not the proper object of one's moral orientation but a characteristic of the being and actions of a person creating and responding to value.

This observation brings us to the really basic moral ques-

---

[6] Cited by Peter Berger in *The Noise of Solemn Assemblies* (Garden City: Doubleday and Co., 1961), p. 176. This statement is not extant in writing; however, Eberhard Bethge regards it as genuine.

tion for the Christian, the morality of his soul or his mind, his being. Bonhoeffer says that there is one thing worse than doing evil, that of being evil.[7] Although being involves doing, being is a more comprehensive category than doing. The immorality of contemporary man is not so much that he drinks, that he lies, that he cheats, nor that he is sexually indulgent. His basic immorality is the fickleness, the irresponsibility, the radical self-orientation through which he regards everything and everybody as subject to negotiation for his (or his family's or his club's) pleasure. The moral crisis of our day is the erosion of the trust, the faith, the reason, and the "affect" of man. Helmut Thielicke has suggested the depth of our crisis in terms of the total rejection of responsibility and guilt in human relationships.

A well-known and very kindly philosopher once told me with every evidence of having been shaken by the experience, of being invited to a tea by a number of students, men and women, at which all kinds of life problems were informally discussed. It turned out that every one of the young men present had had sexual intercourse with every one of the girls present. The fact itself, the philosopher said, did not shock him nearly as much as the matter-of-fact way in which they let it be known and the complete ease they displayed in attitude toward those who in his (the philosopher's) youth would have been called "rivals" or the "jilted" ones. A completely "natural," ingenuous atmosphere prevailed, all quite unproblematical and amoral. The philosopher summed up his impression in these words: To incur guilt is really only the second worst; the very worst is not to be *able to feel* guilt any more.[8]

[7] *Ethics* (New York: Macmillan Paperback Edition, 1965), pp. 17-20.
[8] *Nihilism, Its Origin and Nature* (New York: Harper & Row, 1961), p. 148.

Insofar as a Christian emphasizes the morality of total abstinence, of paying all one's debts, of always telling the truth, of confining sexual expression to wedlock, of tithing, and the like, the Christian identifies Christian faith wrongly with moral action, suggesting the identification of faith and morality. From the standpoint of Christian faith, the critical lapse in these areas is not that one does the wrong things, but that one wants to do them. If one wants to do them, he is evil whether he is able to control his inclination or not. It is, therefore, a misrepresentation to call a man good if all that one means is that he acts in a certain way under certain circumstances. If one is evil at heart—crude, envious, passionless, suspicious, calculating, vindictive—he is still evil in spite of his usual control of himself. Christian virtue is primarily a matter which Jesus called "purity of heart," the singleness and integrity of the affections.

The Christian churches are often also unduly "simple" in their educational approaches because they identify being with action, tree with fruit, and content themselves with emphasizing Christian actions or Christian principles to the neglect of the presence of Christ in relation to the heart or being of Christian people. Against those who identify morality with Christian existence, who say that love is God, it is important to suggest that, strictly speaking, there is a difference between *moral* integrity and *Christian* integrity.

The "principles" of morality, of honesty, dependability, cleanliness, industriousness, or, indeed, the Greek virtues of temperance, courage, wisdom, and justice, are important. But it is a disturbing indication of the coarseness of religious sensitivity that Christian love is so easily identified with a life of "principle" or "principles in action." The peculiar nature of Christian morality is the setting of the life of man within the grace of God in such a way that the primary obligation of the Christian is not to obey principles, to obey laws, to do Christian deeds, or to gain his salvation, but to love his neighbor, to serve his neighbor, and to spend himself in loyalty to God's love in Christ for all his neighbors. The basic nature of this love is to reconcile, not to obey principles or to imitate actions. Love is the constant in all situations. The principles and the specifics of action vary. Reconciliation would mean in some instances a renunciation of principle, in others an adherence to principle. For example, under some circumstances reconciliation may require that one tell a lie, that one compromise a conviction, that one sacrifice his "moral integrity" in order to preserve a "religious integrity." The actual situations within which we live involve us in sympathy, compassion, suffering, and upholding one another in such a way that insistence upon one's own principles often becomes a violation of our love for one another.

There is a telling illustration of this perplexing fact in Dietrich Bonhoeffer's *Ethics.*

Every utterance or word lives and has its home in a particular environment. The word in the family is different from the word in business or in public. The word which has come to life in the warmth of personal relationship is frozen to death in the cold air of public existence. The word of command, which has its habitat in public service, would sever the bonds of mutual confidence if it were spoken in the family. Each word must have its own place and keep to it. . . . When the various orders of life no longer respect one another, words become untrue. For example, a teacher asks a child in front of the class whether it is true that his father often comes home drunk. It is true, but the child denies it. The teacher's question has placed him in a situation for which he is not yet prepared. He feels only that what is taking place is an unjustified interference in the order of the family and that he must oppose it. What goes on in the family is not for the ears of the class in school. The family has its own secret and must preserve it. The teacher has failed to respect the reality of this institution. The child ought now to find a way of answering which would comply with both the rule of the family and the rule of the school. But he is not yet able to do this. He lacks experience, knowledge, and the ability to express himself in the right way. As a simple no to the teacher's question the child's answer is certainly untrue; yet at the same time it nevertheless gives expression to the truth that the family is an institution *sui generis* and that the teacher had no right to interfere in it. The child's answer can indeed be called a lie; yet this lie contains more truth, that is to say, it is more in accordance with reality than would have been the case if the child had betrayed his father's weakness in front of the class. According to the measure of his knowledge, the child acted correctly.[9]

It is naïve to say that a lie is a lie is a lie is a lie, if the lie on the surface (conformity of word with fact) protects a truth in the depths (loyalty to a trust, a relationship). As complicating as this texture of things is, one must hold being and action, forgiveness and responsibility, together if he is to speak of Christian morality. In the cases both of provincialism and of naïveté, it is difficult to identify and to explicate Christian morality because of the peculiar orientation of Christian faith to persons. When a Christian approaches another person to teach him or to persuade him, there is one thing more important than that person's accepting the teaching as true or being persuaded of a position. That is the dignity, the

[9] *Ethics,* pp. 367-68.

freedom, and the honesty which the Christian affirms for the other person. The Grace of God establishes love as the one unambiguous quality of the life of the Christian man. In Christian ethics love as the basic quality of the relationship between one man and another is more important than any other aspect of or within the situation. The affirmation of another person as a human being underlies and undergirds every question as to what the neighbor thinks or believes or how he acts. All teaching and persuading are consequently within love, and the freedom and dignity-attributing character of love remains, whether the neighbor accepts the teaching or not.

The discussion to this point has indicated that the attempt to identify what Christian morality is becomes confused because of the actual life of the Christian communities. We have indicated that in their provincialism and naïveté the churches have to an alarming degree depreciated and obscured the basic reality upon which the moral life of the Christian rests, the grace of God. To the extent that within them the proper quality of concreteness becomes provincialism, that of simplicity becomes naïveness, the churches confuse the very issue they seek to clarify in every attempt to inculcate Christian morality. In the first instance, then, Christian morality becomes a problem because of the unclarity and ambiguity within the Christian communities themselves as to what, precisely, Christian morality is.

In the second instance, there is such complexity to every moral problem that one is tempted to despair of any answer. Indeed, there is no simple moral problem and there is no simple answer to any moral problem. The thoughtful person is sophisticated to the extent that he is shrewd about the intricacies and interrelations of many aspects of every moral problem. He may be sophisticated without possessing an answer, but he cannot be sophisticated without recognizing the complicated nature of the question.

The presence of complexity, however, does not necessarily mean the absence of an answer to or within a problem. As a way of illustrating complexity, let us consider the acute moral problems of the Jewish question, civil rights, sex, and war (the Vietnam conflict, quite specifically), all of which require a response from twentieth-century man. Even in the abbreviated discussion that is possible at this point, it will again be clear why, with a desire for both a good and a sensitive conscience, we are tempted to a grand oversimplification or to a fatalistic resignation to the inevitability of things. The clear moral orientation we seek in order to handle a problem of awesome proportions is as elusive as it is precious. We will return to the question of Christian moral orientation which contains both simplicity and complexity, the sensitive as well as the good conscience, concreteness and universality, in the final section of the chapter. At the moment let us consider, however briefly, some actual problems.

The remark of a person after seeing "The Deputy" contained the sentiments of many: "This is not a play indicting the pope or the Roman Catholic Church. This play is an indictment of mankind." Those of us who participated in the liberation of Europe from Hitler during and after World War II were appalled to discover Hitler's brutality to the Jewish people. At the same time we discovered instances of heroism and sacrifice on behalf of the Jews. Anne Frank's *Diary* and Leon Uris' moving story *Exodus* stimulated the popular imagination and cut the Jewish question into the conscience of twentieth-century man to the extent that he must act on behalf of his Jewish fellowman or die having been less than a man. What was right for a Christian man in Warsaw at the time of the Ghetto incidents? What was right for a Jew who had an opportunity to carry Jewish children from Germany to Israel but against whom the British had a mandate from the United Nations to maintain a blockade? What is right action toward the Jew now in East Germany, Russia, in Syria or Lebanon, in the United States? Is there a specific action which a Christian confession requires? Does the Bible give an answer to the question? Does the church give an answer? Is there an answer in manuals on ethics? Is it enough to care or to pray for the Jews? If one is to do more than pray, is there a particular Christian political or social or economic action which is his to do as a man of Christian faith? What is one to say about the Christian culture of the West before the evidence of the murder of six million Jews?

The nature of the moral problem of man's treatment of the Jews is that there is no "place" of innocence and there is no simple or easy or readily available "right thing" to do. There is no escape through the simple solution of prayer nor through an appeal to the bewildering complexity of the problem.

In the issue of civil rights in the United States the picture is again unclear. There are doctrinaire solutions which are simple enough, "no segregation" or "no integration," or "white power" or "black power." But it would be impoverishing to the meaning of Christian faith and compromising to the many factors involved if one identifies Christian morality with any one of these positions. The response of the white

community in Mississippi and the division within the ranks
of the Negroes on the occasion of James Meredith's march
to the State House in Mississippi are matters of record.
Dr. King's nonviolent demonstrations in Chicago and the
response of persons in the white community there are well
known. These examples can be multiplied almost without
end. There is simply no single available answer for every
Christian who asks: Who is my fellow citizen and how am
I to act toward and for him? There are certainly answers to
this question offered. For example, the biblical literalist suggests an infallible text in the Words of God which establishes
the pattern for human rights and human relations. He may
locate this in the story of the cursing of Ham, Nehemiah's
insistence upon a "clean" community, Ruth's challenge to
religious exclusiveness, Jesus' blessing of the "meek," or
Paul's praise of those who obey God by obeying the civil
magistrates. The biblical spiritualist urges us to obey the
principles under the Jewish Law or the teaching of Jesus.
The traditionalist requires us to obey the law, whatever the
law is. The revolutionary urges us to take the law into our
hands, indeed, to restate the law to serve the revolution.

Again the nature of the problem of civil rights is one which
God does not seem to answer for man, yet one for which
man is responsible before God, specifically in the context of
the churning conflict of the ideas and hopes, the fears and
hates, of men. The urgent moral question of civil rights renders
our simple solutions insipid and our escapist appeal to complexity callous.

For many months people have been speaking of the "sexual
crisis." Perhaps conversation about sex has always been either
carefully guarded or in terms of "crisis." There is some

justification for speaking of a "crisis" in the sixties, however, in view of the public discussion of sex and the changes which scientific progress has made in understanding the nature and consequences of sexual activity. An issue of *Time* magazine around the theme "Sex in the U.S.: Mores and Morality," the wide circulation of *Playboy* magazine, debates between Harvey Cox and Hugh Hefner on the morality of sex, commissions appointed by Pope Paul VI to study the question of birth control, the inclusion of birth control information and material in assistance programs from one country to another, the open and honest attempt by many religious communities to assess "the pill"—all these are indications of the revolutionary or "crisis" dimension of the problem. The basis of the revolution is not that sex is more public, more pleasant, or more available today. The revolution rests upon a plateau of scientific and intellectual accomplishments which make it ninety-five to ninety-nine percent possible for a person to have sex without the danger of pregnancy or of disease. This means that decisions about sex may now be made without regard for accompanying effects or within a cluster of psychological-moral-personal effects which are much less tangible to contemporary man than were the physiological factors of disease and pregnancy.

A young person growing up in the United States today is subjected to diverse pressures which are inevitably confusing. On the one hand sex is used to sell about everything except the meaning of sex. One is sexually stimulated in a propagandistic way by most of what he sees and hears. On the other hand, he is heavily penalized if he indulges or if he indulges outside the written or unwritten rules. Harvey Cox is incisive on the issue. "We have thus fashioned for unmarried young adults a particularly unfortunate combination of emotional environments. They are constantly bombarded—through clothing styles, entertainment, advertising, and courtship mores —with perhaps the most skillfully contrived array of erotic stimulants ever amassed." [10] Within this jungle of manipulative stimulation, the only teaching of religion is often, "Don't go too far!" Again in a naïve way, we allow the thrust of moral responsibility for chastity to be concentrated on the individual person, particularly the female, with very little being done to expose and interpret the moral question of the meaning of sex in relation to humanness and love. One almost feels that the admonition, "thou shalt not," regarding sex has been more important than the "thou shalts" of love, creating a gullible public that is unable to appreciate sex for what it is and which consequently falls for all sorts of *Ersatz* appeals under the guise of sex.

The extent to which we have become brittle and repressive as to sex is illustrated by our defining love in terms of sexual purity or of sexual loyalty. There surely is a relationship between sexual loyalty and love, but not such that love is based on loyalty. This way of putting things reverses the actual relation between them. Love is more complex and more flexible than to be explicated completely in terms of premarital chastity and postmarital loyalty. Chastity and loyalty are extremely important, but they are not identical with love, and until the discussion of love is freed from this identification, it is impossible to derive the power and perspective for chastity

[10] *The Secular City* (New York: The Macmillan Company, 1965), p. 205. The entire discussion, pp. 192-216, is fresh and illuminating.

and loyalty from love. It is precisely at this point that questions of sex become complicated. The real question of human morality is "to love or not to love." When we transform this question into "to bed or not to bed," or "to use the pill or not to use the pill," or "to masturbate or not to masturbate," we oversimplify the basis of human morality to the point of a tragic devaluation of the substance of morality.

The nature of the problem of sex is that God does not speak a clear "thou shalt abstain" or "thou shalt indulge." The one command which is the heart of all others and upon which all others depend is, "thou shalt love." And the one promise within the gospel is, "thou art forgiven." Thus without having a specific answer to the problem of sex, man is able to be honest about the intensity of his affection and desire and yet, at the same time, knows himself responsible for all his sexual expressions in the midst of his own complex motivation and the confusing influences of his culture.

Perhaps there is no need for a further illustration. Yet how can one who is a citizen of the United States when this is being written (1967) make any statement about specific ethical problems without mentioning the war in Vietnam? Is there any problem more agonizing, more complicated, more resistant to solution, about which reliable data are more difficult to come by, and about which simple answers are so irrelevant? It is unnecessary to rehearse the situation in detail. Several aspects of the Vietnam issue which throw light on man's general moral dilemma should nevertheless be mentioned. One is the "impure" status of the present discussion. That is, our question is not whether to go into Vietnam. We are already there. It is not particularly germane to the present question of remaining and on what terms, to talk as if we were considering a fresh issue for the first time.[11] We are sure that the original commitment was not really the present commitment. But we make the present decision as already there, already involved, already "guilty." As irrational as our original commitment may now seem to us, the present rationality which we are able to bring to the question must operate within that original irrationality. Equally irrational is the importance of "saving face" before the cultures of the East.

A second aspect of the Vietnam situation is the negative effect of our effort of liberation upon the people and the land to be liberated. In both World War II and in the Korean action "liberation" and making a people secure enough to determine their own life without terror were words with meaning. The relationship between our warfare and the intention of American foreign policy to assist any people (when asked) in achieving freedom, health, and economic well-being was visible and clear. In the Vietnam situation, however, who the Vietnamese people are or what their desires are is most unclear. Instead of the United States assisting a nation to defend itself against oppression and in the building up of the land and the economy, the United States is the dominant and visible military and political power with more longevity than any native government for the last several

[11] George Kennan's testimony to the effect that if we were now asked to assist Vietnam in exactly the way we are doing, he could conceive of no justification for responding positively, is helpful in assessing the overall situation. Our point is that we are already in Vietnam, and that our presence there now, however wise it may have been at the outset, actually conditions every consideration about withdrawal or the proper "form" of our presence in the future.

years. Perhaps, and hopefully, the election in South Vietnam may clarify what the Vietnamese people want. Quite apart from these factors, however, the data of the Vietnam war speak against a clear and simple solution.

Mr. Eugene Patterson, editor of the *Atlanta Constitution,* visited Vietnam some months ago. Since returning to the United States, he has claimed that the war in Vietnam is the most heroic, altruistic, and self-sacrificing effort which Americans have ever made. Alongside Mr. Patterson's appraisal, one must consider an alternative reading of it, to wit: that the American people themselves are betraying their own revolution by resorting to technological means to destroy crops, land, villages, and people to prove a point against a Communist enemy.[12] In at least one instance there was a report of a Vietcong company being trained unwittingly by the United States. Hardly a day passes without a story of a bombing mistake, or the wounding of many civilians in an effort to kill a few Vietcong. Chet Huntley of NBC news has reported that one of the most depressing aspects of the war is the increasing number of older men and women along with children who are filling the hospitals of Vietnam as a result of the war effort of the United States.

On Sunday, August 14, 1966, the following appeared in an editorial of the *New York Times:*

The Vietnam conflict, which is essentially political, already is overmilitarized and over-Americanized. To send four American divisions into the densely inhabited Mekong delta, where half

[12] The title of an article by Arend T. van Leeuwen, "Can America Rejoin Her Own Revolution?" is most suggestive. *motive,* Vol. XXVI/4, January, 1966.

the population of South Vietnam lives—and where South Vietnamese units hitherto have carried out what is more a police than a military function—could kill and alienate more peasants than it "liberates." Tuesday's tragic air attack in which 24 delta peasants were killed and 82 wounded illustrates the reality of this danger.

The irony in American military plans is that even if they should succeed in destroying most large Communist military units, the clandestine Vietcong apparatus of terrorists, local guerillas, political cadres and rural sympathizers will remain. A popular government in Saigon with Buddhist participation and a program of reform that could win peasant support would be worth ten American divisions. . . . A commitment to endless escalation in pursuit of military victory on the Asian mainland would be a commitment to disaster.

The specific effect of the policy of increased bombing is brought into question as a practical and as a moral issue in an editorial of August 21, 1966.

The bomb tonnage now being dropped on Vietnam each week is larger than that dropped on Germany at the peak of World War II. Civilian casualties and the alienation of peasant loyalty are not the only results when air power and artillery are employed on such a scale outside of large-unit ground engagements. The social structure of the countryside is being smashed; and the Communists may be the ultimate beneficiaries of the wreckage, however the conflict ends.

General Westmoreland's review of "procedures" undoubtedly will be useful. But what is really needed is a major investigation of the whole bombing policy and its effects on South Vietnam. To besmirch the good name of the United States in a program that challenges all moral principles—and may even be defeating its asserted purposes—is to compound horror with folly.

Although we believe that Vietnam represents a major moral

challenge which the people of the United States face today, a challenge in which the integrity and good sense of the American people is at stake, let us not lose sight of the point of the illustration. War, and specifically Vietnam in the sixties, is an illustration par excellence of the complexity of any moral problem. While the simplicistic answers are so irrelevant as to be of no consequence ("Any fight against Godless Communism is right," "Any use of arms by a Christian is wrong." "In Vietnam the United States is fighting God's War." "If General Ky and Ho Chi Minh would accept Christ as Savior, the war would end." "If the Christians of the world honestly prayed for God's answer to the war, he would give it."), one may well be disappointed when he turns to the religious community for illumination. There he will find sharply divergent suggestions, or mushy love with no concrete substance, or a thinly veiled economic or political expediency with no dimensions of authentic love.

Resisting the temptation to analyze the Vietnam problem, let us be clear about the point of the illustration. The question can be put simply enough: "What are we as Christian and American people to do in Vietnam?" The simplicity of the question belies the complexity of the answer. We as Christian people, still less we as American people, do not go to Vietnam with a clear, precise, and practical answer to their strife. God does not, in effect, send us with an answer. But God places a responsibility upon us for the freedom and livelihood of these people as our neighbors.

The nature of the moral problem of war, particularly in Vietnam, is that we are obligated within an ambiguous situation, that we are called to venture ourselves as personal beings within a situation we do not control. The only answer we are "given" is one which comes as we act according to our best moral insight within the complexity of the situation.

If one takes any one of these difficult world problems and tries to answer that problem on the basis of morality alone, he will feel the force of Tillich's idea of a "transmoral" conscience. The "good conscience" must have the right answer upon which to act. The "sensitive conscience" recognizes that there is no one right answer, one law, given in these situations. How is one to combine a sensitive conscience with a good conscience? Only by pushing the moral conscience beyond the sphere of its conflicts to the sphere "from which it must receive its conditional validity." [13] In more familiar terminology, the sensitive conscience drives one to the limits of a moral conscience, to the point where the integrity of one's being depends upon his discovery of "another" who confirms him in his struggle for a good conscience in spite of his failure to achieve it. The good transmoral conscience is a matter of faith, a matter of the grace of God. A sensitive moral conscience is a matter of openness, of capacity to feel, of power and responsibility to act. It is the purpose of all the chapters that follow to throw light on the relationship between faith and action. One of the factors which calls us to the search is the complicated nature of every moral decision, especially when it is made about the most critical human problems. The nature of man's moral dilemma is that he himself must give an answer he cannot discover, that he himself must somehow combine a sensitive and a good conscience, that he

[13] Paul Tillich, *The Protestant Era* (Chicago: The University of Chicago Press, 1948), p. 149.

himself must reconcile what he affirms in faith with what he is able to accomplish in action.

ELEMENTS OF AN AUTHENTIC ANSWER

The issue between the mother and the student, between the churches and the world, between the advocates of the new morality and those of the old, between the editor of the *Atlanta Constitution* and the editors of the *New York Times* may be that of mutually exclusive commitments, in which case these points of view conflict but never really meet. It may be, however, that the positions are in dialogue with each other, there being elements in common between them, with a different "mix," a different proportion and emphasis, a different cast to the surface of the positions. Although we are inclined to think that the latter is the case, we will suspend judgment on the question until we are clearer about the elements which any tenable morality must include.

PRINCIPLE AND CONTEXT

One of the most lively discussions in religion at the moment is that between the contextualists (ethics of the situation) and the legalists (ethics of principles or laws). Although this way of stating the contrast gives verbal advantage to the contextualist (being a contextualist is all right, but who wants to be a legalist?), we are in agreement with James Gustafson to the effect that context versus principle is a misplaced debate in Christian ethics.[14] It has been an error in the

---

[14] Gustafson, James A., "Context Versus Principle: A Misplaced Debate in Christian Ethics," *Harvard Theological Review*, Vol. LVIII (1965), pp. 171-202. Also reprinted in *New Theology No. 3,* published by Macmillan and edited by Martin E. Marty and Dean C. Peerman, pp. 69-102.

ghetto orientations of theological positions that the principles of the legalists are misconstrued by the contextualists, and the situationism of the contextualists is misconstrued by the legalists. Principles do not necessarily falsify or manipulate the situation; the situation (or context) is not devoid of principles. Any answer which is valid must involve principles *and* context, indeed, principles *in* context. Principles operate in a situation in two ways, as guiding factors in the conscience and thought of an individual moral agent who must act in a situation, and as ingredients in the texture of a situation, as operative within other persons involved in the situation. Decisions about premarital sex or abortion involve the principles by which one lives and a fair assessment of the principles which operate in the lives of the other people involved. A decision about Vietnam involves an individual in relation to his own principles and the principles by which the Vietnamese people, the other people of the East, and the people of the United Nations act. Integrity of moral action is achieved only through a response both to one's own principles and to the principles of other persons. The image of a Christian who derives principles from outside the situation which he carries into the situation is misleading. The moral question, even about principles, is their meaning within a situation of interpersonal conflict or difference. If a principle is not viable within the actual, concrete, particular situations of life, it is so much salt that has lost its saltness, a drag on man's effort to be moral.

On the other hand, context or situation does not exclude principles. The demands which twentieth-century life place upon man have forced us to cast off particular principles at many points. But a shift in principles, abandoning one which is irrelevant or brittle for one which is more adequate to the

38

particular conditions of life, is not, in itself, to become "unprincipled," a moral anarchist. Against an unimaginative identification of love with many principles, we are discovering a meaning of love which, while active through principle, is normative over any principle. In Bonhoeffer's illustration it was clear that the principle of truth-telling meant one thing as conformity of word with fact, and quite another on the level of loyalty to a relationship. Loves decides if truth is to be told and what kind of truth. The whole existence of a person, his thoughts as well as his love, is involved in this decision about truth-telling. Yet who would accuse the student of abandoning the principle of truth-telling? On the contrary, he seems to have discovered a difference between various principles and to have become a moral agent upon the deeper issue of who he is as a person among persons. Here a student acts in terms of principles that are adequate to the complexity of the situation, but he is not without principle. The principles of loyalty, of individuality, and of honesty become relatively more important than those of a particular kind of truth-telling. One is willing on the surface to be a "liar" in order to be loyal to a deeper question of morality and of humanity. Love makes this possible because love both creates the guilt of acting against principle and the insight that one principle is more important than another in this case. Love is not a principle but an existential reality which weighs principles in full cognizance of all the dimensions of an actual situation.

As much as we desire and cultivate detachment, we live in concrete history, through actual decisions; and whatever morality we finally embrace must be relevant not so much in heaven or between the intense episodes of existence, but in, with, and for a situation of our decision in relation to a complex set of data and a number of other people. Whatever one accepts as an adequate Christian ethics must recognize the place of principle *and* of context. If our life is in "meeting" one another, our morality is in the substance and relevance of our principles *in* situations of meeting one another. We refuse ultimate commitment to principles which keep us from engagement in the general dance of human relations as well as to such an ecstatic absorption in the dance that our sensitivity to principles is dulled. There must be, however obscure and unpopular, a morality of principles in context.

LAW AND SPONTANEITY

In the story of the young ruler (Matt. 19:16-30; Mark 10:17-31; Luke 18:18-30) the contrast between the law (ethics for the ordinary) and the momentary (ethics for the exceptional) is vivid. One might read the story as a radically exclusive contrast between that which is valid for *any* time (law) and that which is valid for *one* time (spontaneity). Indeed, one might go further and construe the difference between Judaism and Christianity as that of a radical choice between incompatible ways of life, law and gospel. To do either, however, would "fix" the interpretation of an issue against much evidence of the Bible and of history.

As for the young ruler, law is a security of an objective sort, a full statement of God's demands which sets forth the conditions upon which one might receive eternal life. Law on these terms becomes a part of a contractual agreement. If the ruler satisfies the conditions, he has a claim on God for eternal life. The ruler's desire for his own salvation had blinded him to the needs of his fellowman. But this is surely not the proper meaning of law in the faith of the Hebrews. Law, more properly speaking, is teaching within a covenant of deliverance (grace) and election (responsibility). Law is an expression of the will of God to assist man to live his history in response to God's speaking and action. The parable of the young ruler is more an exposure of the ruler's misinterpretation of the law than a stricture against law.

As for the Jewish-Christian conflict, there is gospel in the faith of the Jews and there is law in the faith of the Christian. There remains a difference between the Christian and the Jew which should not be minimized. Ambassador Goldberg has seen this point. "It is wonderful that Americans are coming to realize that the difference between Christians and Jews is not worth fighting about, but it would not be so wonderful if we became so listless that the difference is not worth keeping." [15] The difference is there but it is not simply that of law against gospel.

Any ethic, to be tenable, whether Jewish or Christian or atheistic, must have a place for law and for spontaneity. Law in this instance is the enactment of rules governing human behavior setting forth rights and responsibilities, and making available to any man the wisdom of others who have faced similar problems. The purpose of law is humanization, not regimentation. Thus the law may be criticized and changed in response to new situations or to new moral insights. Rather than being opposed to spontaneity, law is the vehicle through which we develop the wide range of sensitivities which enable us to be spontaneous in a new kind of "moment." Indeed

---

[15] In a speech to the 50th anniversary convention of the National Jewish Welfare Board, quoted in *The Christian Century*, May 18, 1966, p. 641.

spontaneous action may be harmful as well as helpful. A person whose orientation has been illuminated by law is more able to act helpfully in a situation than is the anomian or antinomian. A person who makes a fresh moral discovery in an "extraordinary" situation will seek ways in "ordinary" life to share this discovery. What is fitting at the moment is extremely important in Christian morality because faith can only be exercised in present history. What is fitting at one moment, however, is related to what is fitting at other moments. What is fitting in relation to one person at a moment is related to what is fitting in relation to a lot of other people at the same moment.

Those who oppose law or spontaneity constrict either law or the moment for the benefit of the separation. It is helpful to isolate them for analysis and understanding. It is also helpful to combine them for synthesis and understanding. To isolate two persons from the whole human family at a moment or to cut one moment from its context in the temporal flow of overlapping moments is a bit of historical obscurantism, unless through these two persons other persons are understood, or through this moment other moments are understood. The rich, interrelated texture of life in history is such that law, as teaching, and spontaneity, as that which is fitting for the moment, are held together. What life joins together let man not put asunder! Teaching which is not conducive to spontaneity is false teaching. Spontaneity which refuses kinship with other moments of spontaneity is false spontaneity. Any morality which claims credibility must provide moral illumination both for the ordinary and the extraordinary situations of life.

SIMPLICITY AND COMPLEXITY

It has been admitted that there is a proper kind of simplicity in life, and this against those who have a simple answer to every question. It is also granted that there is a proper kind of complexity, and this against those who use complexity to deny all simplicity. The person who has never seen the complexity of things is naïve. The person who insists that there is no simplicity is cynical. Our moral problem is to delineate the proper spheres of simplicity and complexity and to indicate how these are related in human life. Alfred North Whitehead speaks of all actual occasions as having a physical and mental pole. In an analogous way we might speak of every moral issue as having both a simple and a complex dimension. The way of insight is to see the proper place of each rather than to expend one to benefit the other.

At certain critical moments in life all the mitigating and complicating factors become recessive before the burning simplicity of the question. If the clergyman asks the question, "Do you take this woman to be your wedded wife?" then "Well, yes and no" is an inadequate answer. One may simply say at that point either "yes" or "no," however many times he may have weighed things and considered "maybe yes, but" or "maybe no, but" before. If one is becoming a citizen of a new country, he is expected to have considered the various possibilities and have concluded in utter simplicity that this is the country for him. If the doctor explains to the patient the nature of the cancer and the possibility of an operation being successful, say, fifteen percent, the patient must eventually give a simple answer, asking for the operation or choosing to take his chances without surgery. In most instances the data are ambiguous and complicated, prompting a "yes and no" response rather than a clear "yes" or a clear "no." The data are important and will have stubborn influence no matter what decision one makes. But the data do not dictate the decision. The decision is a simple and clear one made by a moral agent who takes a risk in the context of the complexity of the people and issues involved. To be sure, we are prone to postpone the risk as long as possible, and to reduce it as much as possible. In spite of the effort, we are not successful. Being a human moral agent makes the risk inevitable.

An adequate morality will take account of both these factors and assist one to identify one issue in which a simple answer is indicated, and another in which an openness to complexity is the right response. In general the basic and ultimate issues, such as whether and what one loves or fears, one's understanding of and commitment to God, the primary quality of human existence which one shares, are simple. The preliminary or secondary matters are complex. The myth within which one lives is a simple and clear question, whereas all other questions within this life orientation are complex. Pure love is a simple actuality, but it is infinitely resourceful and complex in its enfleshments. We do not suggest that there is a code way to isolate simplicity and complexity, but that the texture of life contains moral issues which themselves contain simple and complex dimensions and which are in temporal polarity with one another. One is not given a simplicity to impose upon complexity, nor a complexity with which to confound simplicity. One is given a rich content of historical existence within which he, as an actor, must make a decision. One is given a spectrum of simplicity-complexity within which he is called to say a simple "yes" in one instance, a complex "yes and no" in another. A viable Christian morality will help him see both the distinctiveness and the interrelatedness of these qualities.

Is There a Viable Morality in Christian Faith?

Part of the burden which the contemporary church must bear is the kind of fixed and brittle interpretation which previous generations have given to faith and morality. The received picture of faith was that of a person with strong and literal assent to the words of the Bible and of the creeds. That of morality suggested a set of moral laws, Victorian version, which one must observe to be a faithful disciple of Christ. The fact that these virtues would pass muster for a conventional, prudent, and successful citizen of the twentieth-century Western world more neatly than for the disciple of Jesus in the Gospels or the writings of Paul seemed not to bother anybody. To an embarrassing extent the Christian forces of the West became so comfortably related to the established orders of political, economic, social, intellectual, and military powers that the revolutionary, prophetic, and creative forces of the Christian vision were stilled. H. Richard Niebuhr has traced this development most ably. He suggests the coziness of the relationship in familiar words. "A God without wrath brought men without sin into a kingdom without judgment through the ministrations of a Christ without a cross." [16] Less familiar are other words of his, "To be reconciled to God now meant to be reconciled to the established customs of a more or less Christianized society." [17] Almost completely

[16] H. Richard Niebuhr, *The Kingdom of God in America* (Chicago: Willett, Clark & Company, 1937), p. 193.
[17] *Ibid.*, p. 181.

unfamiliar are the words of the contemporary German writer Gerhard Szczesny. "In these countries, where Christianity still holds uncontested sway over the cultural facade, the Christian idea has degenerated into trivial moralism, which has no religious superstructure left at all, and in lieu of it projects the Babbitt ideal, of the man who is in all ways healthy, normal and satisfied with himself, the world and providence." [18]

Since World War II, however, this "received" world view has collapsed, stage by stage. Much of the ferment and strife of the fifties and sixties is to be understood in terms of man's mixed response—of weakness and of strength, of resignation and of creative activism—to the collapse. A revolution has taken place, and there is no way to live except in relation to it. For religion this means that whatever creed one says must bear fruit in terms of a trust that enables one to live the revolution. For morality this means that whatever moral principles or laws one holds must produce the fruit of courage and love in the most threatening moments of the revolution.

As exposed and full of danger as man's search for an authentic morality in a postmodern age is, we honor and identify ourselves with that search. Whatever value there is in Christian faith which calls an event of the past to memory, or sketches a picture of the future, is secondary to the form of Christ's incarnation (Presence) in our present history, a form which creates the possibility of honesty and therefore may be trusted, a form which heals and reconciles and therefore frees man to creative and venturesome activities, a form which loves and therefore reveals one's neighbor to him as a fellow-

[18] Gerhard Szczesny, *The Future of Unbelief*, trans. Edward B. Garside (New York: George Braziller, 1961), p. 78.

man, a form which has structure and therefore engages the mind to articulate this meaning in the warp and woof of life.

For many persons the search for a present integrity is impeded by the memory of the Christ event and the hope of the eschatological event. This is certainly understandable if the virtues impressed upon the student (attendance, tithing, no smoking, drinking, or sex) became more important than love, compassion, and courage. If the received culture is archaic and lifeless, brittle, and repressive, one must attack it with all his resources to achieve a morality with depth and power. Gerhard Szczesny has depicted this person most vividly.

As soon as man begins to live consciously, as soon as he ceases to be guided by imported norms and instead conceives a desire to do and strive, wish and want in terms of his own insight, so that he may bring his life, as he feels, into an intelligible relationship with all reality—when this happens any lack of harmony between motive and deed, idea and configuration, the believed and the known tends to become intolerable. Having arrived at this stage, man must either find new motives while continuing to act as before, or new forms of action while retaining his old motives. That is, he must either find a new way to accommodate his existence to the Christian idea of faith, or rebuild his existence on a non-Christian basis. In the end there is nothing left for him to do but to bring everything that he does, hopes or wishes into harmony with what he has come to believe is the nature of the whole.[19]

In the words, "he must find a new way to accommodate his existence to the Christian idea of faith," is an indication of the effort which is made in these pages. For if the actual content of a Christian ethic is both relevant and positive, flexible and substantial, one should consider that ethic as a

[19] *Ibid.,* p. 79.

possible one for himself. We are led by study and thought and life to discriminate within the "received" image of Christian faith and to discover a Christian existence that not only opens one to honest participation in present history but also imparts power and light within that participation.

The clarifying and constructive insight which Christian faith imparts to morality is the simple insistence that there is only one demand placed upon all men who would be authentic and mature, and that is to love. The only thing that is always, unambiguously right for the Christian is to love. On the other side, the only thing that is always, unambiguously wrong for the Christian is the failure to love. Everything else, literally everything, is secondary. If one fails to love, he fails as a human being. If one fails in any or all other things and succeeds in love, he succeeds as a human being.

A second strength of Christian ethics is that it is a faith ethics; which is also to say that the strength of Christian faith is that it is an ethical faith. The claim of the Christian is that his action is within the context of God's action, but that God does not compromise or act in place of man. Likewise, man is not asked to play God, to do the work proper to God. Christian ethics becomes a viable and exciting possibility because on the one hand it continuously holds man to the responsibility of being human and a fellow-human, with all other considerations secondary, and, on the other hand, it affirms the graciousness of the ultimate, of God's action toward all men, as the reality-environment within which all men act.

As paradoxical as it may seem that a sharp delineation of the responsibility of God and that of man should be the ethical fruit of an incarnational faith, that is exactly the situation. The incarnational form of manifestation is an indication of the inextricable relationship between God and man and of the reality of love. At the same time, Christian faith maintains that God is God, not man, and man is man, not God. With this recognition, the Christian believes that man is created to love *and* that he is loved. Without identifying his love with God's he nevertheless can accept God's love as God's and the opportunity for human love as a peculiar responsibility of his own life.

It is our conviction that there is a viable morality with rare qualities of radical honesty and courage and goodwill within Christian faith. But it is our task to show more clearly how that is the case. To move in that direction let us have a look at the first-century proclamation of the new age by Jesus and his interpreters in the New Testament.

II

Confronting a New Age

Therefore, if any one is in Christ, he is a new creation; the old has passed away, behold, the new has come. (II Cor. 5:17.)

You know that those who are supposed to rule over the Gentiles lord it over them, and their great men exercise authority over them. But it shall not be so among you; but whoever would be great among you must be your servant, and whoever would be first among you must be slave of all. (Mark 10:42-44.)

MEMORY AND PRESENCE

One of the most arresting sights in Jerusalem, Israel, is the *Yad Vashem,* a memorial to the millions of Jews who were systematically killed in the 1930's and 1940's. Over the entranceway to an exhibition held there in 1966 were the words of the Baal Shem-Tov, "Forgetfulness prolongs the exile; remembrance is the secret of redemption."

The quotation from the Baal Shem-Tov, accentuating "for-

50

getfulness" and "remembrance," suggests the importance not only of what is to be remembered but also what it means now to remember something. It is characteristic of both Judaism and Christianity that we find our place in the present by remembering the past—and that a particular focal point in the past is the center of meaning. In a general sense we may say that a Jew is one who remembers Exodus-Sinai; a Christian is one who remembers the Christ event.

"Remembrance is the secret of redemption." This kind of remembering does not mean just a factual memory. The memory of faith is symbolic memory, which brings the past into the present by opening a present situation to the dynamics at work in a previous event. Factual memory describes the past. Symbolic memory invokes the past in such a way that there is present participation in the reality remembered from the past.

If, after an analysis of the present difficulties of Christian ethics, we turn to the past, to the remembering and re-presenting of a particular focus in the past, we are following the structure of Christian faith itself. For this faith is inescapably bound up with one particular place and time of history—with the figure of Jesus Christ. At the same time, we are not turning to the past with the claim that the meaning which for Christian faith focuses in Christ is inaccessible elsewhere. To say this would be to confuse factual memory with symbolic memory. We simply affirm that from where we stand, the inescapable concrete focus of meaning is Jesus Christ. For someone of Jewish faith, much the same ultimate meaning is focused in the memory of Exodus-Sinai, but there will be characteristic differences of emphasis. For others, there is no concrete historical center of meaning.

The historical relativity of our situation often obstructs conversation between different standpoints, but conversation is nonetheless possible. Indeed, our conversation with ourselves labors under the same difficulty, for we stand both in the focus of Christian meaning and in other, sometimes contradictory, patterns of meaning. The approach to faith through a particular memory can serve as a useful reminder that faith is not a harmonious part of culture, and that we need to be alert to the contradictions in our commitments.

There have been times when faith seemed to be a harmonious part of culture, and when its truth seemed naturally, almost obviously, true. There are still many who live today in a cultural setting in which Christian faith seems to have this quality of self-evident superiority to other options. But increasingly, even in the culture which has been most pervasively shaped by it, Christian faith does not seem obvious today. It comes to us as something different from the standards which we find for ourselves in the world, and yet which calls us to find ourselves by taking seriously the concrete situation of the "other," the neighbor, in his "world" and ours. In this respect our situation is much more like that of the first Christians than was the situation of an earlier generation. For, to an earlier generation, at least more than for us, the truth and acceptability of Christianity were in harmony with their cultural standards as a whole and thus more obviously "true."

It is an advantage to our understanding and choosing faith to see how different the claim of faith is from our community-accepted cultural standards. Yet the separating out of Christian faith from cultural forms that formerly seemed to be Christian—the realization that our common standards of goodness or love, our common idea of God, and our common ideas of what is right in personal achievement and in standards of social relations, are not "Christian"—this separation does not of itself bring us to an understanding of faith.

Faith is always given as men use their freedom, and its coming as well as its departure will always share in the unpredictability of freedom. We can see, however, that a great part of our own contemporary difficulty lies at the level of awareness. The Christ of Christian faith is a reality at the edge of our possibility of awareness. He is not wholly beyond, for he comes into the lives of men and can be known. But such knowledge is not a secure possession; we cannot guarantee its permanence, and it is not a knowledge which we can control.

Our life continually tends to shut out the awareness of that which is at the edge of our possibility of awareness, the awareness of the ultimate; for the Christian, the awareness of God in Christ. Faith almost always finds a tension between its necessary involvement in the patterns of profane, secular life and its more fundamental encounter with the ultimate ground of its being, God. This tension is at the basis of the alternation between sacred and secular, between worship and the world, which appears almost universally in religion. But our contemporary Western world has so shaped our understanding and imagination that it has come close to shutting out all sensitivity to or awareness of the holy. So pervasive is this secular thrust that Mircea Eliade speaks of it as a "second fall." "From the Christian point of view, it could also be said that nonreligion is equivalent to a new 'fall' of man—in other words, that nonreligious man has lost the capacity to live religion consciously, and hence to understand

and assume it." [1] Although there are some who believe that this loss of awareness means that we must abandon the "holy" or the "sacred" in Christian faith, we believe that the New Testament can help to open our eyes to the possibility of recovering the true meaning of awe in the presence of God.

"The edge of our possibility of awareness"—this means that faith calls on our selfhood to extend itself to its limits—of sensitivity, of commitment, of action—and that as the self extends itself to its limits, it will find itself upheld, not by the structure of its own achievement, but by grace, by acceptance. It means that God's gift is not to be measured by any fixed external standard; it can be received by each man at his limit (of intelligence, of freedom, etc.), whatever that is. As we shall try to show later, the spectacularly visible "limit situations" of the saint or martyr have real value as parables, as symbolic enactments of the extension of the self to its limits. But they are not models of Christian action, because they contain the temptation of "heroic" concentration on the self, and because the limit may equally well be found within very prosaic and conventional situations. The "edge of awareness" does not require of all a heroic disengagement from conventional patterns, but it does call for a radical openness to the holiness that is there at the point where human action has reached its limit.

The tension within the faith between the striving to be genuinely open to the awesome presence of a Holy God, and the striving to bring knowledge of God within the usual limits of awareness, to make it safe by making it like other

[1] Mircea Eliade, *The Sacred and the Profane,* trans. Willard R. Trask (New York: Harper Torchbooks, 1961), p. 213. Cf. the comment on this passage by Thomas J. J. Altizer, *Mircea Eliade and the Dialectic of the Sacred* (Philadelphia: The Westminster Press, 1963), p. 27.

knowledge, shows itself with pathetic and frightening clarity in the history of the church. As we have seen in the previous chapter, the most familiar form of falsifying faith is to make it into a set of religious rules, a secure and predictable morality. The moral distortion, in which a controllable moral obligation becomes a substitute for the full freedom of Christian faith, is the commonest distortion of Christianity in our world, and it is against this distortion that much of the rejection of faith in our time must be judged. To a considerable degree it is rejection of moralism, and has not yet even considered the meaning of real openness to the Holy One.

The Recovery of the Origin

Men meet the reality of God in the present, and the Christian stance toward life is directed toward free and responsible living in the present. This means that, faced with an erosion of faith, those who are seeking faith (whether consciously or not) may and do recover their origin, their foundation, by a new meeting with the present, and that Christ is present to faith and not just a figure of the past. It may even be the case that some of the most genuine movements of recovery of faith are so deeply immersed in making an authentic contemporary response that they cannot identify themselves with the churches, or even with what they understand by the figure of Christ.

Nonetheless, for Christian faith it is characteristic that the seriousness with which God treats human existence is confronted in a decisive encounter with men that took place in a concrete time and place, in Jesus Christ. Faith involves a rediscovery and indeed a re-enactment of this original encounter. Recovery of authentic faith involves a dialogue between the claim of the present and the model encounter in the past. Time and again the roots of the Christian faith have been rediscovered by a fresh meeting with the paradigm or model of the New Testament. Yet no later generation can simply reduplicate the original faith—often as some, especially Protestants, have thought that they were doing this. The meeting with early Christian faith may, however, enable a later time so to restructure its faith that it can freshly express the radical yet concrete openness to the holy that is found in the New Testament. To this recurrent task we now turn, to see whether New Testament faith can illuminate or even counteract the confusion and loss of faith which we find in ourselves and in our own time.

THE END OF THE WORLD

How can one turn or return to the point of origin of the faith which has been so eroded in modern culture? The personal seeker turns toward an immediate meeting with what he can "hear" the New Testament say; the scholar turns his critically trained eye on the records to find out what he can "see." The one stance is immediately concerned; the other distances itself from the religious writings and observes them. Between these two approaches to the New Testament, or to faith generally, there is a long history of tension, and this stress is strongly felt today. But there can be no long-term profit from these two approaches rejecting each other. In our own particular problem, that of a fresh recovery of the point of origin of New Testament faith, it has been scholarly study that has opened up a new avenue of approach, by discovering that the core of the New Testament proclamation is "eschatological," that is, that it expresses its faith in the form of the hope for the coming of the end of the world. Something over fifty years ago Johannes Weiss and Albert Schweitzer forced this realization upon a somewhat reluctant world of scholarship. A great deal of the theological side of New Testament study since then has struggled with the question of what sense a modern man can make of this mythological form of thought.[2]

The New Testament (with a few important exceptions, which apparently do not belong to the earliest period) grasps the reality of God in Christ in terms of the coming of a New Age. Jesus himself also expressed his message in this eschatological form. The background of this way of understanding the ultimate encounter of God and man is in the Judaism of the two or three centuries before the time of Jesus. Here, in circumstances of uprootedness and tension, and at times of actual persecution, there developed the eschatology which provided the thought-forms of Jesus, Paul, and the earliest Church. This form of Jewish faith sensed the tension between God and the world, between the ultimately real and the actually existing, so strongly that it expected the whole fabric of social, political, and even in some sense personal, existence to be dissolved by a direct encounter with the pure reality of God. Such faith finds its fullest Old Testament expression in the book of Daniel; other works, not included in the Bible, such as Enoch, the "Slavonic" Baruch, and some of the

[2] Cf. Albert Schweitzer, *The Quest of the Historical Jesus*, trans. W. Montgomery (New York: The Macmillan Company, 1961 [originally published in German in 1906]); Amos N. Wilder, *Eschatology and Ethics in the Teaching of Jesus* (rev. ed.; New York: Harper & Row, 1950); James M. Robinson, *A New Quest of the Historical Jesus* (Naperville, Ill.: Alec R. Allenson, 1959).

writings from Qumran, also give a vivid picture of this faith.

The form of eschatological thought is mythological and symbolic. In the seventh chapter of Daniel, successive imaginary beasts emerge from the sea in one of the writer's visions, each symbolizing a "beastly" earthly empire; then "one like a son of man" appears, symbolizing the new and unearthly rule of "the saints of the Most High." Details of the symbolism often escape us, but the overall thrust is clear: immense and mysterious forces are grappling in combat; man is not the master of his situation, and God, at the moment, appears to be absent; yet this structure of existence which is so insensitive to the divine justice and love will not endure much longer; God will destroy it and erect a new existence, a real existence, into which he will transform and elevate those who are open to his rule. At the same time this picture of transhuman struggle is presented as a summons to human faith and endurance.

Such faith is usually expressed in bizarre symbols, and it does not strive for our kind of logical precision. Eschatological faith, however, often includes a strong speculative component, a strong drive to know the secrets of the future and thereby to master the insecurity of man. A typical expression of this speculative aspect of eschatology is the attempt to order the history of the past (as in the vision of the four beasts mentioned above) and to show how past history leads toward the great fulfillment. Daniel's speculation about the time of the end was many times repeated in Jewish and Christian eschatology.

It is characteristic of the eschatological faith of both Jesus and Paul, and of the central thrust of early Christian faith, that this speculative attempt to master the events of the future is sharply curtailed. Both Jesus and Paul expected the end soon. Both used a fund of traditional eschatological imagery. But in both cases the thrust of the message is not to put the believer in a position where he is secure because he knows the future, but rather to expose him to the total claim of the divine. Thus the central use of eschatological symbols in the New Testament is a dialectic one in which the immediate referent of the symbol is both rejected and affirmed (the world is to be destroyed and yet what follows this death and destruction is described as a "new world").

Since the symbolic language of faith (in this case, eschatological thought-forms) expresses a human effort to grasp reality as a whole, and since our modern experience makes us sharply aware of the gap between the inner world of human meaning and the outer world of events, some have concluded that symbols really speak only of man's inner world, and that the naïve picturing of God at work, in the myth and symbol of the New Testament, must be reinterpreted in terms of man's inner world; divine powers have to be excluded from any meaning mythical and symbolic language has for modern man. While we agree with the starting point: myth and symbol are expressive of a world of human meaning, we find that the reduction to "inner" human meaning is made in contrast to a specific and too narrow understanding of "empirical events" as the alternative to inner human meaning, and we do not find that divine action is understood in the New Testament as this kind of empirically verifiable event. The reduction of the speculative element in New Testament eschatology represents a different sort of distinction: not between the empirically verifiable event and the world of meaning in which man can live, but between man as creating a world of meaning which supports and affirms him in his effort to be secure, and man as "creature," as planet around the sun, as sustained in life only after and through the death of the security for which he grasps. Thus the language of New Testament eschatology remains mythical, but it is a reduced, non-speculative mythology. As Amos N. Wilder says:

A paradox of biblical religion is that in both the Old Testament and in the New we have to do with faiths that are in a real sense iconoclastic, that is, mythoclastic. A chief feature of both is their rejection of pagan myth. . . . [Yet] the men who gave us the New Testament employed the world pictures and the salvation pictures of their own time to set forth their faith. For the Word of God speaks with the words of men and with the everyday language of men. But the everyday words of men are image-words and the Word of God necessarily employs these.[3]

In other words, eschatological faith in its most central expressions (in the Old Testament as well as in the New) expresses a vision of the transcendent which shatters the patterns of human existence so thoroughly that the mythological patterns which grasp human existence are also shattered; yet the retention of human images (as against a complete silence as the ultimate Word) shows that in this faith God takes human existence seriously and takes it up into his fulfillment of existence.

The Kingdom of God

In the message of Jesus the central term is the kingdom of God. "The time is fulfilled, and the kingdom of God is at

[3] Amos N. Wilder, *The Language of the Gospel* (New York: Harper & Row, 1964), p. 129.

hand." (Mark 1:15.) Jesus proclaims that the New Age is about to be established by God.[4]

As in the earlier eschatological literature, the coming of the Kingdom means that Jesus understands his time to be a time of polarization, a time of decisive and ultimate struggle between God and evil. He presupposes the context of Judaism as his message is addressed to the Jewish people, but the ethnocentric aspects of the coming judgment which sometimes appear in Jewish and in Christian visions of the end fade away. It is not by belonging to a special group that men will be judged, but by the thoroughness and perceptiveness of their obedience. And the image of national triumph does not figure in his words about the future. Rather, so far as it touches on the people's future, his message reasserts the old prophetic theme of judgment on the failure of their loyalty.

The Kingdom is proclaimed by Jesus on a note of joy. This was easily enough seen by those who could understand little else about him. The joy is associated with God's breaking through the barriers of human pride and security in simple, spontaneous goodness. The useless, the failure, the outcast—these hear the note of acceptance by God which those who have made themselves secure in their achievement fail to see.

[4] On the kingdom of God, see the book written in 1926 by Rudolf Bultmann, *Jesus and the Word*, trans. Louise P. Smith and Erminie Huntress (New York: Charles Scribner's Sons, 1934), chap. 2; cf. also Günther Bornkamm, *Jesus of Nazareth* (New York: Harper & Row, 1961), chap. 4; W. G. Kümmel, *Promise and Fulfilment* (Naperville, Ill.: Alec R. Allenson, 1957); the work of Rudolf Otto, *The Kingdom of God and the Son of Man* (Boston: Starr King Press, 1957 [first published in German in 1934]), though it now is seen to be inaccurate in many details, still retains its importance as a basic statement of the balance between present and future in Jesus' proclamation of the kingdom of God.

At the same time, the proclamation of the Kingdom is a call to obedience, a call to respond in total freedom and with wholeheartedness in the same open and complete way that God is seen to be confronting men. The uncompromising and almost unconcerned way in which Jesus sets forth this claim for obedience is a perennial challenge and a perennial frustration to those who read it. The note of joy at the coming of God's rule goes hand in hand with the note of life-in-death, of "losing one's life," of (in what is probably later Christian language read back into the words of Jesus), "taking up one's cross." (Mark 8:34.) "Blessed are you when men hate you, and when they exclude you and revile you. . . . Rejoice in that day, and leap for joy. . . ." (Luke 6:22-23.)

Thus the Kingdom means the "end" both of the outward structure of security which men found in the heritage of their people, and of the inner safety they found in their status and achievement. It is a promise of life, but made in such a way that one can only hear it as at the same time a call to surrender one's life and achievement. As Amos N. Wilder says,

For Jesus the Kingdom of God represented as it always did in the faith of Israel something far more than a condition characterized by moral attainment and moral relations. It was a state in which men would participate directly in the glory of God, would see his face. This is not to say that the Kingdom of God is beyond good and evil in every sense. It is beyond good and evil in the sense that the paroxysms of the divided self are overcome and that the life of personal relations is sustained spontaneously rather than voluntarily. There is no moralism, no law, no calculation of duty, nothing mechanical, no bondage of the conscience, no seal placed on the springs of individuality. . . . But in a higher sense ethics still characterizes the Kingdom in that it is a kingdom of personality, a communion of selves, whose peculiar beatitude is made possible by the combination of liberty and loyalty.[5]

The Kingdom in this sense is still to come, but its power and character are already "dawning," coming into being in connection with Jesus' proclamation. Men confront its reality when they confront Jesus' proclamation and action. "But if it is by the finger of God that I cast out demons, then the kingdom of God has come upon you." (Luke 11:20.)

It seems beyond question that Jesus expected the final end soon, and as such stood in the tradition of Jewish eschatology in which the nearness of the end, as Wilder says, seems to be in proportion to the intensity of faith.[6] We recognize this expression of faith in the reality of God's promise in terms of its nearness as a sign of how deeply human Jesus' action was, so deeply that he shared with his time an expectation that was not fulfilled.

To the inquiring student it is disconcerting to find that the part of the message about the Kingdom which forms its bridge-point for later Christian memory—the part about the place of Jesus himself in the coming of the Kingdom—is the very part which scholarly study has found most difficult to attribute to Jesus himself. He talked about God, the kingdom of God, and obedience to God. The Christian believers talked about Jesus as the Christ, the focal representative of God's action. Already the forms of the Christian message which are presented in the Fourth Gospel show Jesus as expressing his unique relationship to God with clarity and definiteness, though

[5] Wilder, *Eschatology and Ethics* (rev. ed.), p. 210.
[6] *Ibid.*, p. 24.

the attentive reader of this Gospel will see that this assertion is continually misunderstood by those who hear Jesus, and finds real comprehension only later, after his earthly existence is over. Even in John, Jesus' being the Christ is not nearly so obvious as it is usually taken to be. And the first three Gospels present a different picture in which the role of Jesus, though clear to the writer and to the reader, is seldom in the focus of Jesus' own words. When it is, it is often difficult for the careful student to be sure what the original meaning of these words was, or the extent to which they express the confession of faith of the church rather than actual memories of Jesus.[7]

For our purposes we do not need to probe the enigma raised by the scholarly analysis of Jesus' words about his own place in the eschatological drama. This scholarly discovery is another illustration of the paradoxical way in which intellectual discoveries that seem to threaten faith may turn out to make possible a more adequate realization of what faith is. For the traditional way of assuming that Jesus "knew who he was" threatened to put the emphasis on the believer's security resting in Jesus' knowledge. Our clearer picture of the central thrust of Jesus' message confronts the hearer with the full responsibility to decide whether he will entrust himself to this message and this Christ or not. But the person who takes this message seriously does find that it is backed up by the behavior of the man who speaks it. At this point the message of Jesus and the Cross are all of a piece.

[7] The reader may consult the somewhat contrasting treatments of Günther Bornkamm, *Jesus of Nazareth.*, chap. 8, and Reginald H. Fuller, *The Mission and Achievement of Jesus* (Naperville, Ill.: Alec R. Allenson, 1954), chap. 4.

THE FAITH IN CHRIST

But the message of Jesus is not yet the Christian message, which bases itself, in Paul, the Gospels, and elsewhere in the New Testament, on Jesus as the Christ who is known as such by the resurrection. Here, too, the original formulation is eschatological. But the future-oriented eschatological scheme has been transformed by the faith that what men encounter in Christ is itself a decisive eschatological action of God. This faith makes it appropriate to use titles drawn from the hope (Messiah, Son of David, Son of Man), to speak of him who has already come, Jesus. Thus while Jewish eschatology had looked forward to a decisive transformation of existence by God in the future, and while this future orientation is still a mark of the message of Jesus even though the future Kingdom impinges on the present in his words and work, the Christian faith understands the coming, death, and resurrection of Christ as events so fundamentally transforming of existence that they can only be spoken of in ultimate, eschatological terms, as "end events." Yet at the same time existence continues, not transformed. The impact of the decisive encounter with God can be seen only by faith, and the final, inescapable transformation of existence still lies in the future. Thus "believing existence" is existence "between the times," or "in two times." In Christ God struggled with the evil, sin, and death that divert human existence from its true intention, and the power and presence of this victory are there for faith. But the victory cannot be a possession; it does not totally transform existence, for the "old" existence, the existence at a distance from God and in alienation from one's fellowman and from oneself, continues both around and in the believer, and no one can extricate himself from it, despite the pathetically mistaken conviction of some Christians both in very early times (some of Paul's opponents) and down to today, that their faith exempted them from involvement in the universal human condition.

This double aspect of faith is shown in the joining of the believer, in faith, both to the death and to the resurrection of Christ. On the one hand, faith encounters God's victory in the resurrection. Thus Paul expects "the Spirit of him who raised Jesus from the dead" to dwell in the believer, and to open to him a freedom which he did not have before. (Rom. 8:11.). However this may be interpreted from the point of view of the resurrection as a historical phenomenon—and there is a wide difference of interpretation—from the perspective of faith one finds in the resurrection a discharge from bondage to the old existence, and an access to a transforming power which is known to be one with the transformation which God intends. But this new access to life does not set one free from death. It is the correlative to a union with the death of Christ, with his exposure of himself to the full brunt of the forces which resist God's transformation of existence. Thus it is not only the case that the transformation by faith is never complete and must be continually renewed or re-enacted; but also that the more complete the transformation, the more complete the exposure and vulnerability to the destructive forces. Thus the paradoxical dialectic of death-in-life and life-in-death reaches an intense pitch in the eschatological faith in existence "between the times."

THE INTERPRETATION OF ESCHATOLOGY

The rediscovery that eschatology was central in the New Testament was not originally the result of trying to make the

Christian message meaningful in our time, but rather of the outcome of scholarly study. At first this emphasis was resisted by those who wanted to speak to the immediate problems of faith, because the ancient eschatological way of understanding faith was so unmodern and mythological. Second thoughts have shown that, while we have to face the truth in any case, there is actually great depth of meaning and the possibility of speaking powerfully to our own situation in the eschatological form of faith.

It is true that the early Christians and Jesus himself expected the end soon. In this way faith expressed the nearness and total claim of God. This concrete hope was not fulfilled, and its non-fulfillment shows clearly enough that we cannot mechanically adopt the ancient thought-forms of eschatology. Beyond this rather external item, the real difficulties with the interpretation of eschatology lie at the point that eschatological faith is a way of being grasped by the claim of God to all of existence, by the overpowering holiness of God that will not allow any existence to continue apart from him. The difficulty and the fruitfulness of eschatology lie in the fact that it is radical faith.

As we look at what such faith may mean to us we thus put first that this was faith in the holiness, the unbearable greatness, majesty, and power of God. It is possible to believe that the sensitivity to the holy is so eroded in our time that the sense of awe can no longer be central for faith. But we hold that a confrontation with the uncompromising power of New Testament faith can serve to open our eyes to the wonder and joy of awe before the Holy One.

The form of eschatological faith is its openness to the future, and this form rather than any concrete picture of the future is the key to its importance today. God is the God of the future. The call of faith is a call to be open to what is to come (in contrast to the frequent closing-off of life in the forms of the past which one often sees among Christians). Here the memory of the past is brought to mind not as something to which one turns back, but as something which contains the promise through which one can look forward.

Correspondingly, such faith sets men free from conformity or "bondage" to the world in which they find themselves. The powers and authorities of the world are not ultimate powers. Political structures, then as now, seemed to many to be the strongest forces that exist. Without denying their power, the faith in a New Age declared that one need not fear them nor, in fact, obey them when their claim contradicts the claim of God. Equally true is it that the inner powers with which we struggle, the powers which bind the self within itself and prevent it from entering into true community, will be broken and are being broken by God. Freedom from the powers of this world, from its standards and power-structures, freedom to obey God in the light of his superiority to what men honor—this freedom is woven in with the recognition of God as the Holy One. To put it differently, only God is sacred; the world of man's action is secularized, set free from false claims to ultimate loyalty.

Then we may take it as central that this is a faith in which God takes persons seriously. The New Age is repeatedly imaged as a new community, a "holy city," a community in which men can really be open to God and to one another. God's New Age, even though the wiser ones knew it could not be visualized, was presented as the fulfillment of God's purpose to create a new humanity, and this purpose, however we reinterpret it, is a central meaning of eschatological faith.

Finally, for Christian faith the central use made of eschatology was to transform it by affirming that in Christ the New Age is coming into being. The new element in the New Testament faith is that the purpose of God is given concreteness and power because it is seen at work in the figure of Jesus Christ. In him, God comes to grips with the destructive powers of the Old Age, and though these seem to triumph, the New Testament believer knows that faith can see the dawning of God's victory in Christ. The Gospels and Paul largely avoid the descriptive imagery that seems so strange in the "apocalyptic" books. But strange as the visions of the "End" may seem in books which look forward to it as something soon to come, the early Christian faith is stranger still in substance (if more reserved in form), since it believes that despite all the seeming evidence to the contrary, God has created a new situation for men through the coming of Christ, so that the powers of the New Age enter into man's existence newly and decisively in Christ.

To put it a little differently, we can point out that, though in later generations Christians mostly tried to understand Christ by asking what he "is," the New Testament mainly tries to understand him by what he "does," or, better, what God does in and through him. In Christ, they believed, God presented himself to man in such a way that he could confront men most deeply, most personally, most "humanly." In Christ the conflict between God and the power-structures which men create to give themselves security, the conscious aggressiveness which they pour out upon their fellowmen, and the deeply-lying unconscious forces which pervert their lives and distort their relations to one another—this conflict reached its most intense point. Not because God visibly exerted his power to crush these demonic, distorting forces, but because the life and death of Jesus brought to expression a radical self-giving. In a word (a word so watered down that it is hard to use), in Christ God spoke and lived the life of love, not the love which desires and possesses the loved one, but the love of sheer generosity, of spontaneous giving, of self-giving. The "End," the ultimate action of God's creative goodness in the face of the chaos which men have made of themselves and their world; the "End" that judges and condemns what men in all honesty must acknowledge themselves to be; the "End" of that failure of community which was so clearly the result of the long centuries of striving after community both within and beyond the Hebrew group; the "End" as a judgment which goes through justice to acceptance, and which makes an end of human evil by freely opening itself to the needs of those who are destroying themselves and taking on itself, without compulsion or resentment, the consequences of their actions—these are some of the ways in which we may understand the fact that the early Christians saw Christ as the end of an old world and an old way of life. Such faith is protected from sentimentality because it takes judgment seriously; the end is judgment, and through judgment it is fulfillment. By the same token the New Age, the Age in which there is real openness between man and the indescribably great mysterious reality on whom man's existence depends, this New Age is breaking in on men in the coming of Christ and is really there for them if they open themselves to it in trust.

The faith that the New Age is really there for those who

open themselves to it in trust, however, did not mean for them that the past which made the present different, or the present moment itself, offered the presence of God as a secure possession. One could open himself to the new life only by coming to it in complete unprotectedness, in faith, without asking for the security which men so easily crave. Indeed, the tremendous access of new, life-giving power which men of faith received through the death and resurrection of Christ was hidden so far as the mere (non-believing) observer could see. The "world" did not know that its deepest powers had been undermined or cancelled by the quiet working of God's love in Christ. The eye of faith, on the contrary, could see at work, in its own selfhood and in the community which sprang from faith, a new power and a new freedom which is called the beginning of a New Age.

It is the central stress on trust which makes the New Testament faith accessible to us today—not because trust overrules our better judgment and enables us to believe what is contrary to contemporary standards of truth—but because all truth is at bottom recognized by a commitment to that which is worthy of trust. The church as a community that knows the presence of Christ has been subject to a terrible attrition, and we are insensitive to faith in the ways recognized at the beginning of this chapter. Nonetheless, the New Testament faith that newness of life is concretely and humanly met in Christ still speaks powerfully to our situation, confronting us with the option that being human consists in receptiveness, in an honesty about the pervasiveness of the gift one receives through God's goodness. Gerhard Gloege remarks, commenting on Camus' suggestive interpretation of the myth of Sisyphus, which for Camus means that for modern men true life lies in a totally human assumption of self-responsibility:

Sisyphus lives in us all—as a constant threat to our existence. He survives in every heroic attempt to master life in our own strength. He lives in the remarkably resilient mistake of men who will rely on nothing but themselves. Sisyphus will not consider it true that to be human means first of all to receive. He does not believe that man can only act after having received. Consequently he runs the constant risk of betraying humanity into the hands of a barbarism of higher pedigree in the name of man! This barbarism consists in man's self-reliance and self-involvement, man's total surrender to himself so that he is constantly sunk in himself.[8]

The Christian style of life is the style that recognizes the radical nature of faith, that sees man as finding the wholeness of his existence in unprotected trust. It is also the faith that affirms the living presence of Christ in his community. It is from this point that we can approach the difficult problem of the resurrection. The resurrection signifies that the meaning of Christ is not based merely on memory, but that the presence which is remembered is also presently encountered. The affirmation that the small and humble channel of Christ's presence is decisive for existence is made as a confession of faith. It means that here *we* find the ultimate ground of our existence, and that our acceptance and freedom in our present time are received through a renewal of the memory of Christ.

We will have to express our faith in new forms, for we do not understand the world as the first Christians did. Our faith will not be eschatological in the same way that theirs was. But

[8] Gerhard Gloege, *The Day of His Coming,* trans. Stanley Rudman (Philadelphia: Fortress Press, 1963), pp. 292-93.

72

ultimately the affirmation that God did come close to men in Christ making possible for them a new openness to himself must remain today as then a decision of faith. That does not mean it is a blind or arbitrary decision, for there are many ways in which we can come to a better understanding of what it means to choose this faith and to open oneself to this God. And this faith, like any other, must always remain open to question and criticism, both from without and from within. We can see in our own day, far more clearly than some of our predecessors, that faith's communication is "witness," a declaring of where we stand. It is not a proof of the superiority of our position, and Christian faith can take other faiths seriously and see them also as part of God's work; it can see in them real relations between man and God. But taking other faiths seriously does not mean looking for a lowest common denominator in religion. There are real differences in the various forms of faith. Different forms can, at least imperfectly, communicate, and through such conversation we can come to see things in our own faith to which we were previously blind. Still it is the nature of faith to give us a concrete place to stand, to call for our decision, and to help us communicate with other faiths from our particular point of faith. Just as human loyalty and trust involve a deeper dimension of life than observing speculation, so Christian faith calls for the whole self, for the openness and lack of security which Christ himself displayed in his confronting of men. Christians maintain that those who open themselves in faith, in this way, to the work of God in Christ, find that there is something present, both an honest judgment and a life-creating reality by which the foundation of their life is remade.

There is no way to make such a faith wholly "sensible" today, in the world of modern thought, any more than this was possible in the time of Paul. In many ways this faith is an affront to reason—for reason tells us to make what sense and system we can of the world as we find it, while faith stakes its all on a basis deeper than the empirical and visible community of men. But this faith is not destructive of the self or of the mind. Indeed it reaches out into the world in responsibility and love, so that life "between the times" is detached from the world insofar as the world is a compulsive cause of behavior, but responsible to and in the world as the place where, here and now, God has set us to live in love. Christian faith is by its nature a faith which lays a man open to the needs of those among whom he is set. Its grounding in past and future does not mean emptying the present of meaning—for the present is the time when I, in my own concrete circumstances, respond to the claim of life and the world upon me as my response to the ultimate graciousness I see in Christ. Thus the thrust of our encounter with the radical faith of the New Testament is to place us responsibly in the community of persons in which we find ourselves. For us, also, forgetfulness prolongs the exile, and remembrance is the secret of our present redemption.

III
The Encounter of Love

It was the will of the Lord to bruise him; he has put him to grief. (Isa. 53:10.)

Love bears all things, believes all things, hopes all things, endures all things. (I Cor. 13:7.)

LOVING AND BEING LOVED

We have seen that in its beginning, Christian faith was sharply set over against the "world," that is, against the structures of life in society and in the personality in which men find security to assert themselves. The early Christian faith was "eschatological." It expressed its radical opposition to the world in a hope that God would soon abolish, and was in fact in the process of abolishing, the whole network of structures that make up the world, and would soon establish his will as the only reality. We cannot here follow the development of the Christian church as it moved away from the original eschatological form of faith, in which freedom from the quest for security in the world was maintained by the hope of the world's coming to an end. Instead, we shall look at once at the problem of expressing generous love, and see how the expressions of this kind of love repeatedly bring to light once more the radical claim of the original faith as well as its tension with the world.

In Christian faith, human love can only be understood as a response, and not as an independent activity of the self. Of course, this distinction is not always consciously kept in mind. But as we reflect, in a Christian perspective, on what it means to act in love, we see that it means to be set free from one's egocentric concern by acceptance, by being forgiven and upheld in one's existence in spite of one's lack of value. "We love, because he first loved us" (I John 4:19), is the classic formulation in the New Testament.

Love, in the sense of open self-giving, is the reflection of a greater self-giving to which we entrust ourselves. This is true of all fully generous love, and to the extent that our ordinary human relations express this openness, they can become a model by which we can speak of the meaning of God's love. Yet the fragmentary character of our best human responses to the lives around us, the mixed character of those responses, and the fact that they are only fleetingly achieved, all show that we cannot by any means claim that it is sensible to argue from the observed fact of human love to the existence of divine love. There was a time, not so long ago—and it is still reflected in a good deal of religious literature—when it seemed possible to many Christians to move rather naturally in this way from human love as the highest thing in human life to a higher sustaining power, the love of God. This way of thinking was possible because there is a genuine analogy between the intention of self-giving on the human level, and the self-giving which Christian faith finds in Christ, the self-giving which is received as an act of the God who is the ultimate basis of existence. But the analogy is not nearly so complete or comprehensible as it seemed to the period of "liberal" Christian faith.

The intention of openness and self-giving as we find it in human life is too deeply interfused with aggressive or with purely "survival" drives to serve as a base from which an analogous love can simply be attributed to the ground of existence, to God. In other words, in the context of human life, radical openness to the other is a fragment, a partial response instead of the total response it intends to be. Even when it is genuine within a certain limited framework, it can and often does function in another framework of egocentric concern for security. This double reference is easily apparent in the love of a parent for his child. In this relationship there may often be a genuine element of self-giving and openness, an acceptance and support of the younger life which helps to enable the child to emerge from his complete egocentricity. Yet at the same time, from another point of view, this same relationship will be an expression of a tough will to survive, so simple and elemental a will that it may, if pressed, ignore even the most basic human responsibilities outside the immediate relation of the family. Thus a German journalist, looking back on the Second World War, writes:

The time when all order collapsed like rotton wood, when none of the things we call "society" seemed to hold up, not even nation or state, no organization or community, no matter how solemnly pledged, this time of the closing-off of all values, of general collapse, was the time of triumph of the family.[1]

In somber yet moving colors the author paints the quiet, dogged struggle for survival of German women, intent on keeping their children alive and maintaining a remnant of a home for their men to come back to, cleaning up after air raids and searching the countryside for a little food. But this revelation of the power of giving within the small circle of the family was at the same time a stubborn narrowing of forces to concentrate on the one aim of survival, and this fact is tragically made clear by the inability of most of those who faced this struggle to express an openness to life beyond the immediate group of the family, as in the resistance movement, for instance. Yet within the narrow framework there were many actions of profound self-giving, of deep openness to the other life; and while some of this openness and love was associated with Christian faith, much of it was not. This situation in which men and women were pressed to the limits of their capacity makes painfully clear what is always true of human existence—that total freedom to be "there" for another person is only a fragmentary response, and that the very necessities which may call forth a sacrificial openness in immediate relations may and usually do close our eyes to other sorts of demands made upon us.

THE AMBIGUITY OF ENCOUNTER

Thus the day-by-day human relations in which men find themselves provide occasions which bring to light the strange

[1] Klaus Harpprecht, "Plädoyer für die Feigheit," *Der Monat*, No. 172, January 1963, p. 18.

ambiguity of the encounter with another person: most of our meetings with others are superficial occasions in which we screen our real selves and do not look very deeply into the other. When we do confront another person more seriously, the relationship has deep organismic roots—the encounter involves the competitive struggle for survival, the drive of sex, the defensive association of the pack, but also the protectiveness of the parent for its young, a curiosity which reaches out to explore and know, the give and take of equals. Within this complex of relationships there may be—perhaps most evident in the "model" of the parent-child situation—a fragment of intention (sometimes of decisive action) of pure openness, of "being there" for another, of taking him seriously as a person—an element which far transcends the purely organismic level and reaches to personal responsiveness. Though it is only expressed in broken fashion, this element of spontaneous "thereness" can be creative in human relations, setting the accepted one free from his anxious involvement in himself and giving him in turn the possibility of freedom to be truly responsible. Yet this moment of generous love is tragically ineffective, partly because even where it is present, it tends to be present only in one frame of reference—for instance, in the immediate circle of the family—and its very intensity in one frame of reference often serves to blind the self to other claims, to others who are equally "there," as our illustration above has shown.

Furthermore, it is painfully easy to mistake our image of the person who is "there" for the person whom he wants us to see. Generous love is often sentimentalized and weakened by this blockage between the two who are trying to communicate. The difficulty is apparent in all types of encounter. How often a child is offended—perhaps permanently alienated from a parent—by the inability of the parent to see him as he finds himself to be—grown, able to live his own life, perhaps in many respects wiser than his parent! Some of the most painful examples of this barrier to real personal meeting are coming to light now that non-Western cultures are beginning to articulate their response to the coming of missions from the churches of the West. What was understood from the Western side to be an act of self-giving often appears from the non-Western side as arrogant and aggressive, and contemptuous of the real person in the non-Western culture.

The "right" is not all on either side in these cases of nonrecognition. A person who resents being treated like a child may actually be a child; on the other hand, a person who understands himself to be deeply open to another may be asserting his self in dozens of unsuspected ways. For the moment we note only the fact that people being what they are, there is a permanent "built-in" obstacle to love in the difficulty of confronting, not the person whom I am prepared to see, and not even the person who understands himself to be there, but the person who *is* there confronting me.

We have set forth these "structural" limitations to full openness before mentioning the most obvious difficulty—namely, that we do not choose to be open. Consciously or unconsciously we treat the one whom we encounter as if he were an "it" rather than a "thou," to use the distinction made familiar by Martin Buber.[2] Our closing-off of ourselves against the life of others is often obvious and frank enough; at other times it is disguised from others and from ourselves,

[2] Martin Buber, *I and Thou*, trans. Ronald Gregor Smith (New York: Charles Scribner's Sons, 1958).

the more readily because the claim of the "other" is so disturbing. In a world in which the prevalent themes of sensitive writers are the loneliness of man, his isolation of himself within himself, the violence which men work upon one another, and the twisted, uncommunicative nature of such openness as does exist, it seems unnecessary to describe at length the refusal of men to be open to one another. But at least this can be said: no matter how fully we may understand ourselves as functioning in terms of deep organismic drives, or as fixed in social situations which compel us to act in a certain way and blind us to the possibilities in other lives and other ways of acting; no matter how grim and inexorable the portrait of human inhumanity may come out as it is painted by the modern artist; no matter how sharply we may have to reject the rosy picture of human nature that we find in the literature of an earlier generation; nonetheless, this situation in which we set ourselves against one another is not "natural." The very passion and clarity with which our own generation can see and speak of this human condition is itself a rebellion against it. We all resign ourselves to some degree to living within ourselves, to closing off or fighting off the claims of other lives—yet the possibility of openness remains to haunt us, whether we regard it as a fragment that is tragic in its incompleteness, or only as a vision of something that does not really exist at all.

FAITH AS RESPONSE TO THE
AMBIGUITY OF LOVE

What can be made of this situation from the standpoint of Christian faith? We can approach an answer by noting that the tension between the structures of self and society which lock us up in ourselves, on the one hand, and the claim of the "other" on my self and action, on the other, is the situation out of which the eschatological hope of Early Christianity arose.

Insofar as we can speak of it as a response to a human problem, the Christian faith in Christ is a response precisely to this situation which we see so clearly today. But it is a response which transforms our understanding of the situation, since it affirms that in Christ God has come to grips with our situation, and done so precisely in terms of spontaneous, self-giving love. In Protestant faith today, a vigorous discussion is raging about the extent to which faith is concerned with the historical Jesus, as against its being concerned purely with the Christ who is proclaimed in the Christian message. We do not need to go into this discussion here, except to point out that from the point of view of our question—the question of understanding the encounter of love—both sides in this theological discussion are agreed that in faith in Christ we confront, as the ultimate Reality, a love which accepts and forgives us, as Christ enters fully into our situation and makes it his own. One side of the debate about the value of historical knowledge emphasizes that we can find an analogy to faith in the intention of the earthly Jesus. The other side holds that the paradoxical, unpredictable nature of God's love is only fully expressed when we say that we know his goodness only in the proclamation of the Christian message, and that no human goodness, not even that of Jesus himself, can make this paradox of divine acceptance any more comprehensible. But both sides are agreed that Christ and his cross and resurrection have for faith just the meaning we have mentioned: in him we encounter concretely the sustaining and forgiving love of God, which discloses that the fragment or vision of self-giving love is troubling and disquieting precisely because it points to the reality of God's love and indeed at bottom is a reflection of it. As such, what we have called the element of openness in our encounter of others, the moment of being "there" for a "thou," becomes the nearest model by which we can speak of God's action for us in Christ. But it is the Christian faith that the human relationship is not a model but a copy; the living and life-giving standard is God's love, which is free and creative as ours is not.

LOVE AS JUDGMENT AND ACCEPTANCE

If we can confront the meaning of Christ as the meeting with an active, open love which accepts us in spite of our involvement in the structures which alienate us from one another, in spite of the deliberate choice to exclude the other, in spite of the tragic necessity to neglect one person by helping another, then we find that the first meaning of our encounter is judgment. We cannot face that acceptance without finding ourselves condemned and accepting our condemnation, both for our selves as we understand ourselves individually, and for our involvement in the structures which cut us off from the "other." Legalistic Christianity has made so much of guilt and of conscience as the sense of failure to confront an abstract rule, that we may easily miss their deeper meaning of admission of our failure in the presence of a living God, a God who breaks through the structures which imprison us, not by his power, and not by a wisdom which we can predict, but by a humble identification with us in our "lostness," in our inability to come out of ourselves and be open to our fellow. In the face of that act, we can see the cost of our being what we are, and see ourselves without trying to excuse ourselves. In conventional religious language, we can accept guilt, and not only for our own conscious actions, but for the society within which we live as well. We can see ourselves as Isaiah did: "Woe is me! For I am lost; for I am a man of unclean lips, and I dwell in the midst of a people of unclean lips; for my eyes have seen the King, the Lord of Hosts!" (Isa. 6:5.) At this point love is one of the most difficult things to speak of, for the full meeting of God's love as judgment is repeatedly obscured by our fear of seeing ourselves as we really are. What men tend to see in God is either a love that does not really judge, or a justice that makes its demands in terms of some abstract standard—a "law," in the usual religious language. The first emphasis, the transformation of the holy, judging love of God into a soft or casual forgiveness, the "cheap grace" decried by Dietrich Bonhoeffer, is probably the more prevailing attitude in the churches today.[3] But there is no doubt that the other emphasis, the loss of awareness of love in rigid moralism, has played a large role in the past in developing the legalistic conscience and legalistic morality of so much contemporary religion.

The difficulty of speaking of love in such a way as to make clear the seriousness of its power of judgment, without losing its distinct quality as love, points us directly again to the fact that Christian faith does not merely speak "about" love. As God's act of love it presents and celebrates the life, death, and resurrection of Christ. As Christians have confronted the event of Christ, they have discovered themselves not

---

[3] Dietrich Bonhoeffer, *The Cost of Discipleship,* trans. R. H. Fuller (London: SCM Press, 1959; also Macmillan Paperback Edition, 1963), *passim,* esp. chap. 1.

talking about love and judgment, but being confronted by them in such a way that they found a new understanding of themselves as judged and forgiven; and they have found that they were given a new freedom in the encounter. It is the return to the depth and vitality of this event, honestly confronted by the believer or seeker, that has repeatedly rescued the faith of the churches from a harsh legalism on the one hand, and a "cheap grace" on the other.

As we turn from love as judgment to love as acceptance, we see how the New Testament understanding of love gives the full foundation to the view with which we started: that human love is a response, and not an independent activity of the self. The New Testament has many ways of understanding Christ. Common to them all is the presentation of Christ as the expression and actualization of the self-giving of God. Human love is a response to this—a response which is free and personal, yet upheld and sustained by the giving to which it responds.

Among New Testament "buffs" (if the expression can be pardoned), the discussion of love has been focused by making a contrast between two Greek words for love: *agape* and *eros*.[4] *Eros* is the common Greek word for love. It carries the meaning not only of physical desire, but also of love as longing and desire at all levels; thus the word rightly suggests that most human love has the element of longing deeply built into it. We love what we need and long for, whether on the level of basic biological needs, or on the level of companionship, or on the level of desire for beauty and

---

[4] The classic work of Anders Nygren, *Agape and Eros,* trans. Philip S. Watson (London: S.P.C.K., 1953), retains its basic place in this discussion, despite the fact that it draws the antithesis too sharply.

knowledge, or on the level of longing for God. *Eros* serves
for all these sorts of love, and reminds us (as against a certain
type of morality which has tried to isolate physical love as
somehow in a special and lower class) that all these aspects
in which the self reaches out for completion, for something
which it longs for and needs, are related to one another and
are expressions of a fundamental drive of the self to express
itself and become itself. In fact, within one type of religious
faith, these different sorts of *eros* are regarded as steps
leading by degrees to the love for God, so that in the union
with God the self finally loses itself, as the lower levels are
left behind. This way of thinking about love may of course
term it a response, since all love has an object to which it
responds; but it is not necessarily a response to an activity
or giving on the other side. The action lies with the lover,
the seeker after that for which he longs. The many situations
in which a mutual longing is met and fulfilled in love do not
obscure this aspect of love understood as *eros*.

The word-study approach to the interpretation of faith has
been sharply criticized by those who remind us that words are
not used with rigorous consistency, and that meanings are too
complicated to be compressed into single words; they require
whole sentences for their expression. Keeping these criticisms
in mind, we can still see far more clearly into the various
meanings of love by contrasting the *eros*-love just described
with *agape* as that term is used in the New Testament.

In the first place, it is important to notice that the whole
ground from which love is approached is shifted in the New
Testament: *agape* is God's love, and not simply a phenomenon
in human experience. We ourselves interpret the encounter
of love most readily from the point of view of our experience

of what it is to love, and thus can move very easily into an appreciation of *eros*—love which is understood in just this way. Love as the New Testament understands it, however, is grasped by seeing what it means to be loved, and to be loved in one's relation with Ultimate Reality, with God. What the New Testament writers saw in Christ was a love that was not a longing, that did not depend on the value of what was loved—unlike the love of longing or desire, in which love is interwoven with need and with the striving to fulfill oneself. God's *agape* is free to love even that which does not have value; it is able precisely to create value in men who have set themselves against their true function. Insofar as men's love shows the same freedom and openness, it can do so because it reflects the ultimate love which sustains it. The three main forms of the New Testament message, the Synoptic Gospels, Paul, and John, all share this view of God's love:

Love your enemies and pray for those who persecute you, so that you may be sons of your Father who is in heaven; for he makes his sun rise on the evil and on the good. (Matt. 5:44-45.)

But God shows his love for us in that while we were yet sinners Christ died for us. (Rom. 5:8.)

We love, because he first loved us. (I John 4:19.)

In many other ways, often where the word *agape* does not appear (as in the parables of Jesus), the New Testament expresses the faith that God's love is free from the necessity of choosing its objects by their worth, that it is spontaneous in the sense that it is not grounded in the attractiveness of what is loved, and that it is creative in turning itself to those who have no claim upon it, enabling them to become what they are not otherwise free to be—themselves responsible and loving in their encounters with men. This faith in God's love sees God as conferring meaning on the concrete, unique selves whom he loves; he does not love them for a principle of goodness which he finds in them, nor does he receive those whom he loves into his own Reality. He takes them seriously as selves, as persons with whom he shares himself, and whom he accepts as existing in his presence.

The New Testament believers understood themselves as judged and accepted by such a love, and thereby set free for spontaneous openness toward their "neighbors," those who engaged their lives or who might do so if they were open to them. The many concrete commandments about behavior in the New Testament spring not from a fixed system of law or truth, but from the claim of the "other," who has to be taken seriously because he is taken seriously by God—as seriously as the believer knows himself to have been. Thus the primary line of love joins God's love to me, which opens to me a new situation and a new understanding, to my response to the person who confronts me: "he who does not love his brother whom he has seen, cannot love God whom he has not seen." (I John 4:20.)

It is important to notice that while Christian faith finds the fullest expression of such love effectively reaching men in Christ, this same structural pattern for understanding love is found in the Old Testament as well. There, too, love is made concrete in a historical event, and is an expression of God's spontaneity and freedom. The close relationship between Jewish and Christian faith is deeply reflected in the fact that some of the most perceptive and thoughtful analyses of *agape* have come from Jewish scholars.

The Christian thus finds God's accepting and renewing *agape* in Christ, but he recognizes that another may find a different focus for a faith with a pattern very similar to his own. He recognizes, too, that there really exists a great deal of generous human love that does not think of itself as responsive to a decisive divine event of acceptance or deliverance. Such love may be aware of its "history," in the sense of remembering the persons whose support and faith made its own freedom possible, or it may not even have this awareness. In any case, one who finds his own freedom from his past in his judgment and acceptance by God in Christ is misled if he is tempted to deny the presence of the same love where it is not thought of as a response. From the point of view of Christian faith, it will be natural to affirm that all spontaneous, outgoing love has its ultimate root in God. But it will also be natural for the Christian not to make this affirmation in an argumentative spirit, as if the genuineness or validity of love could be tested by its awareness of this its ultimate source. On the contrary, he will be glad to see whatever he can of sensitive, courageous openness to the "other," and at the same time strive to make clear, perhaps in words, perhaps not, that his own commitment is to the center of spontaneous love that he finds in Christ.

It is important to be clear that when we speak about the *agape* of God in Christ we are not speaking in the same way about love as we are when we speak about openness and generosity in human relations—though the two ways of speaking are not unrelated. When we try to understand ourselves simply as persons in community, we can see that free openness to the "other" can occur, and we can learn something about the circumstances which are most favorable for it. From this point of view, openness will show itself to be one function of the self among others, and it will be clear that normally the elementary biological and social needs will have to be satisfied as a condition for the appearance of openness or spontaneous love. But when we speak of God's goodness in Christ, we are speaking of something like a mathematical limit, or a mathematical infinity. This way of speaking of love is an affirmation of faith about the way in which the Beyond, the ultimate, confronts us in Christ. It is a way of saying that beyond the small, temporary, and separate acts of openness that we do encounter, there is an ultimate and definitive goodness which encounters us in Christ and which radically relativizes all other goodness.

This way of understanding the situation can easily be criticized by those who think it does not claim enough. From within the faith, there will be those who say; if you admit there can be a real openness to the "other" without Christian faith, you have given up the centrality of faith. Correspondingly, the critic from the outside may say: if I can have this openness without faith, then I don't need faith. To this we can only reply that the question is not whether you can "have" openness, or how much you can have, but how that openness is to be understood and whether it may be transformed by the recognition of its ultimate ground. What the Christian affirms is that self-giving love, which we find to be only a fragmentary possibility, at best, is nonetheless the ultimate ground of existence insofar as that ground can make itself known to men. In any event Christian faith is not concerned to prove that "its love is better," but to examine its life to see whether it is actually expressing the response to God's love which is implicit in its faith.

LOVE AND THE STRUCTURE OF "THE WORLD"

Thus we come to a more serious difficulty. It appears that in life as we experience it, complete and spontaneous openness to the "other" is a partial response. Christians affirm that they encounter such a love as the transforming basis of existence. Yet it does not appear that their actions manifest this love with clarity and distinctness. In Christians, too, free, spontaneous generosity is a fragmentary response; and this is so not just because the inner struggle with the "old Adam" continues, but also (as we have seen above) because the structural situation of men is such that we cannot be open to all at once. How do we move from an honest recognition of the ambiguity and imperfection of all our human responses to a grasp of how action arising out of Christian faith can reflect the gift to which faith responds in Christ? Or is faith after all purely a matter of how we understand ourselves, without any reflection in how we act?

These are disturbing questions, and their uncomfortable quality has sometimes pushed Christians into answering them too hastily. Sometimes the attempt has been made to prove the long-term beneficial effects of Christianity by showing the good effects on men and society which it has had. Others have taken the opposite turn and said that Christianity is not intended to make any change in society, and that its effects on the individual are purely inward. Each of these extreme views implies certain assumptions that are incorrect. On the one hand, the view that the meaning of Christian faith, or at least its value, can be read off from its historical effects assumes that men's conscious choices can determine the future pattern of society and of history. In point of fact human history does not show such continuity of intention. What is begun as

91

one sort of activity is absorbed into another; what is begun with one intention may continue as the same activity but be driven by another intention. Christian missionaries who worked, along with others, to raise standards of health as an expression of their faith did not realize that their activity would be a significant contribution to the population explosion! Thus we are not in a position to control history over long stretches of time. Quite apart from other factors, this actual situation prevents us from demanding that any given sort of long-term results flow from Christian faith. To this observation we can add one which is more closely related to the encounter of love itself: if love is an act of freedom and aims to elicit a freedom of response in the other, it seems impossible to demand that it always produce a given sort of result.

On the opposite side, those who stress the inwardness of faith forget that faith is bound to love, and that love in the Christian understanding of it is a relationship that issues into action. They misjudge as well the involvement of the self in the structures of society, if they think that the "real self" is some purely inward thing.

We can try to arrive at a more adequate statement of the possibilities if we return to the fact that early Christianity was an eschatological faith. Those first believers found that they had been approached by a power which called into question the structures and patterns within which they lived, a power which they described in apocalyptic language as the breaking in of the end-time. Yet this new presence did not change the outward structures of existence. We take an example from Paul. He describes the openness which breaks over the structural barriers of his society in this way: "There is neither

Jew nor Greek, there is neither slave nor free, there is neither male nor female; for you are all one in Christ Jesus." (Gal. 3:28.) But—disconcertingly to our modern mind which wishes at once to establish permanent and stable "good" structures —Paul also says this: "Only, let every one lead the life which the Lord has assigned to him, and in which God has called him. . . . For neither circumcision counts for anything nor uncircumcision. . . . Were you a slave when called? Never mind." (I Cor. 7:17, 19, 21.) The new reality makes possible a confrontation of the "other" in his humanness, but it does not put an end to the structures themselves. Whatever is new in the Christian attitude toward these structural patterns of historical existence is new because of the freedom to encounter the "other" across these lines. Furthermore, though Christian faith in turn creates its own structures—a church, Christian patterns of behavior, Christian education—these structures are not the thing itself, and the Christian exercises the same freedom toward them that he does toward other created structures. In both cases, the freedom of love is not a permanent thing which he "has," but a free response which he makes (or fails to make) on specific occasions. Such actions cannot be built into an enduring structure which will perpetuate their intention—even though we inevitably, and rightly, try to do just this. The really open, spontaneous act of love is called forth by a concrete situation, and may in turn call forth a mutual response which will "better" the situation. But if love is really open it does not demand this "chain reaction" or depend upon it. In other words, just as the first Christians saw the whole overarching structure of the world as "overcome" by faith, and found themselves delivered from this structure to be open to those formerly barred off from them, so the act of spontaneous openness in each small case abolishes or transcends the structures in which it acts, so far as openness toward the "other" is concerned, yet it must also treat these structures seriously when it comes to concrete action resulting from this openness.

We may illustrate from a conversation narrated by the East German pastor, Johannes Hamel:

It was evening, a few days later. My young visitor looked anxiously about before he asked, "Is anyone else listening? I would like you to warn a certain Miss X. There are plans to involve her in conversations which will tempt her to express reactionary political views, in order that she may be fired from her job."

"And who are you?"

"I am a functionary of the Party."

"And why don't you warn the girl yourself?"

He looked silently at the ground. Finally he said softly, "Because I'm afraid for myself."

Soon we were in the middle of the Sermon on the Mount, and then at Matthew, Chapter 10: "Do not fear those who kill the body but cannot kill the soul. . . . Are not two sparrows sold for a penny? And not one of them will fall to the ground without your Father's will. . . . Fear not, therefore; you are of more value than many sparrows."

"If that could be true for me," he said finally, "then I would be helped." [5]

About this sort of conversation Hamel makes the following comment:

Then we found that here and there a few of us were beginning to talk to half and full Marxists with love. With love—that means

[5] Johannes Hamel, *A Christian in East Germany,* trans. Ruth and Charles C. West (New York: Association Press, 1960), p. 44.

undiplomatically, in all frankness and freedom, yet not self-righteously or moralistically. And almost everywhere where that happened we saw that the evil spirits stole away and the sea became still. In the place of their dialectically grounded desire to liquidate us (for the moment largely in rhetoric) came human respect and the assurance that they wouldn't do us any harm because we were really "good honest people" whom one protects and defends. Then, here and there, something quite different occurred. Suddenly the mask, which looks so deceivingly like a real face, fell and revealed a helpless man who sinks under his load of sin and guilt, and who clings to the Christian who has treated him with a bit of love, who hasn't lied to him like the others.[6]

The possibilities and limitations that are expressed here are regular characteristics of the open encounter between persons. Such an encounter may open a new depth of response, but it does not create a stable environment which will bring security to either party. The encounter takes place by the discovery of the simple humanity of the "other," often at the cost of profound courage and risk. The risk of love is highlighted by the situation in which the encounter cited above took place. But this risk is inherent in all true openness. It is a weakness of the conventional interpretation of love in the churches that it does not clearly see this; love is spoken of as if it were exercised from a position of security. That is why a situation like that described above can more clearly reveal the situation of all of us. From it we recognize that we are not inherently "masters" of the structures within which we find ourselves.

Acts of love thus cannot be understood as aiming to create structures to protect the loved one from the assaults of the world; often rather they ask him to expose himself more fully

[6] *Ibid.,* p. 25.

to them. It is true, of course, that protection is the intention of love in some circumstances. But the use of the "parent-child model," valuable as it is in other ways, can seriously mislead us by giving us a much too uniformly protective notion of what loves tries to do. This does not mean that "the world" becomes a purely negative category from which one cuts oneself off, or submits to, or fights against. "World" is in fact not a category of objective reality, so that there are certain objective, definable things that are always "world" or certain acts or desires that are always wrong because worldly. "World" is rather a name for those structures or patterns in which we encapsule ourselves, shelter ourselves from the claim of faith and love, and it is only insofar as we do this that the term can be applied. If the pattern in question comes to be the vehicle of full personal encounter, it is lifted from its meaning as "world" and becomes part of the "new world" of faith.

LOVE AND TIME

To illustrate this point we will choose the pattern or structure of continuity in time. This structure is fundamental to most of what we call "world"; our reactions of defense are built around the project of making a continuous whole out of our lives. Most commonsense wisdom has this goal—to pick out recurrent features of life and predict how one can behave to take care of them or, rather, to take care of oneself in them. In one way spontaneous love means being freed from this matrix of continuity in which one is striving to build for oneself a secure place, and we customarily express this freedom from time by speaking of the "moment of encounter" to describe the real meeting with another person. Yet such freedom is concerned with continuity in its own new way: the confrontation with another person as a full self, making his claim upon us, makes us see *his* life as created to form a living whole, a continuity. It is this aspect of love which saves it from being a purely momentary thing, and enables love to take a continuing responsibility.

It is true enough that this perennial situation of the meeting of two persons produces an almost inevitable distortion of freedom; the vision of the other's life as a continuous, meaningful whole leads us to express our concern in ways which try to provide a protective, stable structure in which the "other" can live. The simplest example is the economic one: love recurrently tries to enhance the life of the other by making his economic situation better. Doing this has a symbolic meaning; it is a way of taking the other person seriously as a whole person, of saying to him who he is. But our usual human tendency is to see the protective side of this sort of expression of love as the real intention. A remark of John Wesley will make the point; his rather quaint eighteenth-century language will not obscure the contemporaneity of the problem. Writing about the rights and wrongs of a father's making financial provision for his family, Wesley says that it is legitimate: "To establish these (i.e., the family) also in a position whereby they may with, not without, their diligent labor provide for themselves when he is gone hence." [7] The thrust of loving concern is to create a favorable environment for the "other," but Wesley sees the danger of overprotection. The facts that the particular problem does not confront us as

[7] John Wesley, cited in George C. Cell, *The Rediscovery of John Wesley* (New York: Henry Holt, 1935), p. 374.

urgently (nowadays society takes more responsibility for our families than it did in Wesley's day), and that Wesley tries to solve the problem with a somewhat rigid general rule (leave the family some money, but not enough that they won't have to work) do not conceal the penetrating insight into a real tension in love, the tension between protection and freedom.

But the tension can arise only because love is not a momentary response, but is precisely the intention of being there for the other in the living whole, the continuity, of the other's life. It is in the structure of continuity in time that responsible love expresses itself, and not just "in the moment." True, involvement in the continuity of time means a gamble: we never know how things we start this year will look a year from now. We may intend to free our children from the strains and stresses of our economic struggle, and end up by making things too easy for them—the danger that Wesley saw. But the action of love inevitably reaches into the structure of continuity in time because that is where it finds the "other" for whom it is concerned.

From this example of the structure of continuity in time, we see that the openness of love requires a double movement toward those environing and inward structures which we call "the world": a movement of detachment from them, in faith, as one disengages himself from "the world," and a re-engagement in the world in love, as one acts with what understanding he can muster in the encounter with the "other," to affirm the other's life in the actual situation he is in.

RESULTS OF LOVING ACTION

So far we have not answered the question, how much difference in actual action does Christian faith make? Does spontaneous, generous love change things? From what has been said above, the direction of our answer is clear: the free generosity of *agape* is not capable of being built into a stable pattern in society; it cannot guarantee cumulative results. In other language, the kingdom of God is not present and cannot become present in the structures of society. But this does not mean that love is purely inward. Framed in their history, men yet have freedom. They may respond in love to the love which sustains them, and as they do, they will be set free, however imperfectly, from the past, from the structures which have made them what they are, to reach out creatively toward an "other" for whom they accept responsibility. Such a response acts with the intention of eliciting a similar response. That may or may not happen. In any case its freedom cannot be condensed into a permanent presence. Spontaneous love may redeem situations, but it cannot by its nature guarantee the future. Thus such love does open new possibilities, and there is no definite limit that can be drawn to say this or that is impossible. Yet the structures of the "world" continually reassert themselves, as they will always do in this actual structure of human existence within which we find ourselves. The perfectionism which believed that Christians could be extricated from this involvement has repeatedly been disappointed. To this problem of the concrete expression of love and its results we shall return, from several points of view, later on, for it is the core of the problem of this book.

Here we sum up by saying that if it is true that in Christian faith we believe that God takes our concrete existence with utter seriousness, though we find our freedom only by a detachment from our own existence, so it is also true of one's love for his neighbor, that it is expressed through taking the neighbor's concrete situation seriously as the place where the "other" is really to be met. The freedom of faith is given together with the freedom of love—the freedom to make a courageous venture into the future. The awareness of the coming of God does not leave a man isolated in the presence of God, but exposes him to the persons with whom he finds himself. It is the willingness to take men's needs concretely, humanly, that leads Christians to become involved in enterprises that soon grow away from Christian faith. The prospect of this kind of result should purge us of utopianism without discouraging action. Christian love repeatedly breaks the set patterns which it finds, as men seek fresh and more adequate ways through which God's love may come to expression now.

IV
The Dialectic of Faith and Love

I have been crucified with Christ; it is no longer I who live, but Christ who lives in me; and the life I now live in the flesh I live by faith in the Son of God, who loved me and gave himself for me. (Gal. 2:20.)

So faith, hope, love abide, these three; but the greatest of these is love. (I Cor. 13:13.)

The Loss and Recovery
of Faith and Love

Authentic Christian action is thoroughly human as only love can be. It opens itself to the real human presence it encounters. It "affirms" the other person; love does not directly affirm either a religious truth or even faith itself. Such an understanding of love we have tried to set forth in the previous chapter. Now this emphasis on the "humanness" of the Christian life among men raises a basic question about love. Does openness to the "other" imply faith in God? Or is it a way of acting which can be understood without regard to religious roots, even though the man of faith regards it as a fruit or, rather, an aspect of faith? The question is made the sharper by the fact that openness, generosity, and spontaneous love do exist apart from any conscious rooting in faith and are often profoundly understood within a purely human perspective.

We approach this question with the assumption that both faith and love are easily lost or replaced by substitutes, so that the task of understanding them is not simply a matter of being clearer about things that we already know in our commonsense understanding. Rather, speaking of faith and love means trying to grasp realities that push us to the limits of our selfhood, realities that cannot be possessions. Thus, in speaking of both faith and love, we are not so much speaking about things that we have as we are engaging in a quest, looking for something we do not know, while also speaking of what we partly know. We are, in other words, searching for a recovery of faith and love, not because these once existed firmly and are now, in our secular time, slipping away from us (though this is true in part), but basically because these realities continually slip away from us. The quest for faith and love is the quest for authentic humanity. Yet authentic humanity is not an available commodity, but a reality which we know and are only at those moments when we are most geniunely alive; and even then it remains a mixture of present reality and vision.

We further believe that the quest for faith and the quest for authentic human life cannot be compartmentalized or separated. Those who recognize the quest for authentic humanness as a religious quest, and those who do not, have much to learn from each other. Our own searching is indebted to many who would not think of their quest as a religious one. Indeed, any honest student of the meaning of faith and love in the contemporary world finds as much or more that is relevant for his task in the work of men who are indifferent to traditional religion, or even hostile to it, as he does in the "visibly" religious writers. Thus the modern writers and artists who throw the most light on faith are often not at all "religious" writers.[1] Yet we still affirm that "authentic humanness" is not a self-contained category, that it involves an openness to and for the encounter that can make existence new, the encounter with God, and that it comes to be real in a "being reached" by God and not just by a searching for him.

Within the framework of such a conviction, the quest for a recovery of faith and love may move in two different directions. One direction stresses the awareness of God, who makes possible the new existence with one's fellowman; the other direction stresses love as the concrete responsibility through which God is met and served. Seeing how these two directions reinforce or contradict each other will help us understand the question with which we started: whether love needs to be understood as a religious act.

THE LOSS OR DEATH OF GOD

A distinction which will help us in understanding the issues at stake in the recovery of faith and humanity is the distinc-

---

[1] For example, see Stanley R. Hopper, "The Problem of Moral Isolation in Modern Literature," *Spiritual Problems in Contemporary Literature* (New York: Harper Torchbooks, 1957), pp. 153-70. First published in 1952.

tion between "achievement orientation" and "receptive orientation." The exclusion of the holy from our consciousness is related to the heavy value which our culture places on "achievement orientation," a stance in which the self is striving for mastery, trying to reach a goal. Success in the common meaning of the term, and also the whole pattern of intellectual work, are "achievement oriented"; the popular image of the scientist as someone who has power over what he works with is to this extent true, that all intellectual work shares in the "achievement" structure. It is possible to lessen the competitive pressures of this achievement orientation, but it is not possible to evade this fundamental structure of work. Thus the call for a recovery of awe before the Holy One is a call to stand against the dominant achievement orientation of our values, to explore a realm that can be known only by receptive orientation, by a stance in which the self allows itself to be open, to be acted upon, to be moved to a deeper plane of existence. From this point of view, worship is akin to the deepest creative experiences, which "come," which "happen," rather than being achieved.[2] We shall return to this "achievement-receptive" contrast later in connection with openness to the "other," but for the moment we shall note that the dominance of the achievement orientation contributes to the decay of personal encounter as well as of worship. Morality may be understood purely as an achievement, but openness to the other involves both passive sensitivity and action. Thus, worship is akin to those aspects of personal relation in which the self is receptive, in which something "comes" from the other

[2] Cf. Abraham H. Maslow, *Toward a Psychology of Being* (Princeton, N.J.: Van Nostrand, 1962), for a rewarding discussion of this subject; the "achievement-receptive" typology above is taken from Maslow.

which—to however limited a degree—transforms the life that receives it.

The central question thus is whether, within the receptive orientation, the dimension of religious faith can still be recognized as authentic, or whether the erosion of religious tradition has gone so far that it is more adequate to deal simply with an analysis of human existence and regard what used to be called faith as one way of describing a facet of human existence. We hold that the dimension of faith can still be affirmed with authenticity, and that the pattern of alternation or dialectic between faith in God and love to men is the adequate expression of Christian faith, despite the erosion which it has undergone. At the same time we think that a modern man of faith needs to be aware of how much he has in common with those whose quest for authentic existence cannot find expression in religious terms, or in the language of faith. He needs to be aware, too, that in many ways faith is simply a facet of human existence and can be quite adequately understood as such. Nonetheless, a modern man of faith affirms both the reality of God and the possibility of taking him into account in our understanding of faith—God is not so wholly transcendent that nothing can be said about him.

One way of seeing this issue more clearly is to relate the dialectic of faith and love to the question of the "death of God." This is an ambiguous phrase. It may mean the death or sterility of the prevalent cultural and traditional forms in which faith is expressed, including the ways of understanding God. In this case, faith still reaches out to God even though he may be beyond reach.[3] On the other hand, the term,

[3] The first resolute theological confrontation of this issue was Martin Buber's *Eclipse of God* (New York: Harper Torchbooks, 1957), first pub-

"the death of God," may mean that God himself is involved to the uttermost in the very changes which have made him unavailable, and that the cultural decay of the religious dimension is at bottom an expression of the profound change whereby the transcendence of God has passed wholly into the immanence of Christ.[4] In this case the Christian may indeed still speak of faith, but it is no longer faith in God; it is faith directed toward the Christ who is paradoxically to be manifested precisely in the darkness of present existence. These two meanings of "the death of God" are basically quite distinct, though the second, more radical one includes most of the substance of the first. Both have in common a resolute turning toward the world and away from traditional religious forms.

Both these types of criticism of traditional faith are right in saying that we live in a time when the established expressions and practices of faith are called into question and need reformulation—and some may simply have to go as no longer meaningful. Both perspectives are right in saying that the only future for the life of faith lies in a deeper engagement with the world (see the next chapter!). The profound transformation that is required of faith may rightly be described as nothing less than death and rebirth. Even so, it is not appropriate to speak of the death of God. The life of love in the world still calls for the dialectic of faith and love, and

lished in 1952. Cf. Gabriel Vahanian, *The Death of God* (New York: George Braziller, 1961), and *Wait Without Idols* (New York: George Braziller, 1964). A thoughtful discussion of the theme can be found in Thomas W. Ogletree, *The Death of God Controversy* (Nashville: Abingdon Press, 1966).

[4] See esp. Thomas J. J. Altizer, *The Gospel of Christian Atheism* (Philadelphia: The Westminster Press, 1966), and Thomas J. J. Altizer and William Hamilton, *Radical Theology and the Death of God* (Indianapolis: The Bobbs-Merrill Company, 1966). Our discussion is directed particularly to Dr. Altizer's development of the theme.

faith encounters reality, a reality which, though we may not speak of it traditionally, is the reality traditionally known as God. Three aspects of our rejection of the "death of God" are as follows:

First, both perspectives on the "death of God" undervalue the meaning of occasions of celebration. The alternation of life between the sacred and the profane as it was known in earlier societies was taken over into the traditional pattern of alternation between worship and life in the church. This pattern is severely eroded today, and it may be that many of its traditional forms will have to be abandoned. But the point of letting them go will not be to eliminate the movement of concentration of energy which celebrates the joy and mystery of life and of the God who gives and claims life—the point of the change will be to allow inauthentic and rigid forms to fall into the background so that genuine occasions of celebration may emerge. Many of the critical judgments passed on the church, and many of the proclamations of the death of religious forms, miss this basic point. Though we recognize and indeed throw into focus the disastrous effect of separating the life of faith from the life of the world, we continue to use the word "religion" in a positive sense in order to keep in view the continuing validity of occasions of celebration.[5]

Second, the rejection of traditional theology which maintains that we must turn away from talk about God because our traditional talk about God confuses the God of Christian faith with the metaphysical God of another realm of reality, makes

[5] Cf. Thomas C. Oden, *The Community of Celebration* (Nashville: The National Methodist Student Movement, 1964), and Walter Harrelson, "Social Science and Biblical Perspectives on Man," in *America and the Future of Theology,* ed. William A. Beardslee (Philadelphia: The Westminster Press, 1967), p. 164.

an important point. There is no final theological formulation, and modern men are largely closed to any realm of reality "beyond" this one. In this sense the old metaphysical God is dead. It is also true that biblical faith primarily speaks *to* God and not about him, and there is a constant danger that the God about whom we speak will be an idol, a God whom we think we have gotten under control. Nonetheless, it is ultimately frustrating to adopt the view that the language about or to God and the language about the world have nothing in common. Precisely the recognition of the erosion of the Christian vision in our culture can become a potent reason for trying to recover a more adequate way of speaking about God.[6]

Third, in many ways the most significant challenge of the various programs associated with the phrase "the death of God" is that of the radical theology which retains faith but directs it to "Christ" or "Jesus" rather than to "God," in the conviction that the old transcendence is now no longer meaningful except as a form of repression. Here the dialectic of faith and love is resolutely maintained; faith is not dissolved into humanism. The vision of the death of God represents a quest for a radically new form of faith based on the "coincidence of the opposites." In Christ, Spirit has passed completely into flesh and thus faith must be directed wholly to the world and not to God. A full response to this theology would carry us beyond the scope of our present purpose. Our central

[6] Cf. the important articles by John B. Cobb, Jr., "From Crisis Theology to Post-Modern World," *The Centennial Review,* VIII (1964), 177-88, and "Christianity and Myth," *The Journal of Bible and Religion,* XXXIII (1965), 314-20, and the somewhat contrasting treatment of Helmut Gollwitzer, *The Existence of God as Confessed by Faith,* trans. James W. Leitch (Philadelphia: The Westminster Press, 1965).

The Dialectic of Faith and Love

criticism of it is that it operates with too rigid and absolute
a dialectic, in insisting that the old transcendent has passed
totally into the immanent. This emphasis on total change,
making the previous forms of faith wholly inauthentic, represents a serious attempt to recover in our time the meaning
of radical eschatology as it appears in the New Testament.
As such it stands in a long line of radical theologies which
have been restless with the fragmentation of our experience,
with only glimpses of meaning, and not total redemption.

These radical theologies, including the present one, play a
very health-giving role in the life of faith, in exposing the
half-way character of "main line" forms of faith. At the same
time they live not independently, but by dialogue with a style
of faith—for which we opt—which is more able to accept
the fragmentary and broken character of existence. Granted
that such acceptance means compromise, it also means a fuller
ability to enter into the variety of existence. In particular,
the rejection of "God" in this theology is in good measure a
rejection of the elements of form and structure which in life
stand in tension with the elements of energy. But any ultimate to which men give their loyalty must embody not just
the aspect of energy ("love"), but the aspect of structure and
form ("justice") as well.

THE RECOVERY OF THE HOLY

The one direction for the recovery of faith and humanity is
a quest for the "holy" or the "sacred" in a world which has
flattened the awareness of the holy to the point where it seems
to be no more than a moral obligation or an aesthetic pleasure.
On this line of seeking, we must find ways of letting the
awesome "otherness" of religious awareness come to direct

109

expression again. We must find ways of rediscovering, or better, of allowing ourselves to be grasped by, that ultimate awesome sacred presence, the "holy," or in Christian language, the Holy One.

Within the Christian tradition one of the most striking dimensions of response within a recovered awareness of the holy is the movement for liturgical renewal. The conscious, corporate encounter with the holiness of God is the form of this concern. As against the emptiness of so much traditional worship, liturgical renewal seeks to help us rediscover our true being in the presence of God.

Suggestive for our purpose is the emphasis of the liturgical movement on liturgy as *action,* and corporate action.[7] The recovery of the wonder and joy of the presence of the Holy One comes in part through an overcoming of the dichotomy between the freedom of inner feeling and the achievement orientation of most of our action. In worship we are introduced to action which is not achievement-centered, as the central events of faith are "re-presented" and as we participate in their presence and reality. Just as significant is the emphasis on the way in which the action of worship, if it is real, must lead into action in the world. The interplay between the action of worship and action in the world is disclosed in the way in which Protestant Christians have been rediscovering the meaning of the disciplined community, in which both sorts of action *can* stand in a conscious tension and alternation with each other. Of these Protestant developments the best known is perhaps the one at Iona in Scotland, within which

[7] Cf. Dom G. Dix, *The Shape of the Liturgy* (Westminster: The Dacre Press, 1945), chap. I; J. A. T. Robinson, *Liturgy Coming to Life* (Philadelphia: The Westminster Press, 1964).

the moving spirit has been George McLeod. A different sort of disciplined venture out of worship into the world is represented by the German evangelical academies.[8] The primary direction of the quest for renewal of the urban church is directed toward action and expression in the community of men, but this is joined with a quest for a recovery of the meaning of worship.[9]

We have touched on only one dimension of the quest for a direct recovery of the holy within Christian faith, and we shall not here look at other aspects which are equally important, such as the various lines of attempting theological renewal. But it is a striking fact that the quest for deeper openness to the holy often reaches beyond the limits of the Christian tradition. There are many people today who cannot see a really religious dimension in Christian piety, and many of them find a powerful awareness of the divine in Asian religion. This interest in Asia, as a reaction against the loss of true sensitivity to the holy in Christian, and particularly Protestant, faith, finds notable expression in America as early as Emerson, and the interest has increased sharply in our own time. A colleague tells us that he has never failed to observe a positive reaction to Zen Buddhism among his students; the reflection of Zen themes in J. D. Salinger is well known, and an interest in Asian religion has been shown by many other critical and creative thinkers, such as Arnold J. Toynbee, Aldous Huxley, and W. T. Stace.

[8] Cf. George McLeod, *We Shall Rebuild* (Philadelphia: Kirkridge, 1945), and Franklin H. Littell, *The German Phoenix* (Garden City: Doubleday and Company, 1960), esp. chap. 5.
[9] Cf. George W. Webber, *The Congregation in Mission* (Nashville: Abingdon Press, 1964), and Gibson Winter, *The New Creation as Metropolis* (New York: The Macmillan Company, 1963).

Similarly, in scholarly circles there is today a widespread interest in archaic or primitive religion, among anthropologists and students of myth as well as among students of the history of religion. For all their variety, the studies of archaic religion mostly make the point that it is more serious than the religion of modern man; the archaic man allows his life to be determined by his faith in a totality that does not prevail among modern men.[10] While many of these studies do not concern themselves with the problem of faith in our time, they imply that we have lost something that ancient man, or primitive man, had, namely, religion itself, the awareness of the sacred. From this point of view, what Christianity needs is precisely to rediscover that it is a religion.[11]

All this is relevant for our purpose in that both these movements—the movement for recovery of awareness of the holy within the church (as in the quest for a living liturgy) and the reach beyond, or against, the Christian tradition into Asian or other religion—are attempts to break out of the achievement orientation that is so deeply built into our culture. They tell us that if we find that something is wrong, and react by feeling that we must "do something about it," we will only aggravate the moralistic distortion of our faith. What we need is nothing that we can do, but something that happens to us, in our awareness of being judged and ruled by God. The

[10] We mention here the important work of Mircea Eliade; cf. his *The Sacred and the Profane* (New York: Harper Torchbooks, 1961; first published in German in 1957) and *Cosmos and History: The Myth of the Eternal Return* (New York: Harper Torchbooks, 1959, first published in French in 1954). Cf. G. van der Leeuw, *Sacred and Profane Beauty* (New York: Holt, Rinehart and Winston, 1963) for a study of the roots of art in archaic religion which makes clear that its seriousness does not exclude the elements of play and game.

[11] This is a central thrust of the work of Mircea Eliade.

word "religion" may be assigned a negative meaning by some who speak for this quest, if it is identified with the institutional forms of religion, but this is a quest which puts the highest value on the substance of religion, the awareness of the sacred.

THE RECOVERY OF AUTHENTIC LOVE

The other line of searching evaluates "religion" very differently. It seeks to recover authenticity through and beyond the encounter with the neighbor. Here the weariness with an empty and shallow religiosity forces the seeker to be suspicious of the attitudes and practices of religion, especially the traditional focus of religious action, the church. Because religion has become a compartment, isolated from the rest of life and artificial, it cannot be redeemed by recovering its vitality in terms of a conscious or direct encounter with God. "Religion" for this quest represents everything that is man's creation or achievement in his religious life, man's development of a tradition, a pattern of action—all of which has the effect of protecting him from the necessity of confronting his real life with freedom and responsibility. While the first line of seeking tries to sharpen the character of "holiness" by making us understand its awesomeness and distinctive power, the second quest looks into ordinary life to find within it the possibilities of ultimate commitment. This quest recognizes that rebellion against religion may be a more authentic act of faith than participation in it, for religion may become an armor that protects men from the uncompromising claim of responsible, sensitive obedience in their actual situations.

The church and worship recede into the background in this interpretation of Christian faith, and the focus falls on the human situation. This re-focusing on man in his concrete situation is undertaken not to accommodate faith to man, but precisely for the opposite reason: to confront men with the authentic challenge of the gospel. Herbert Braun's formulation, "God would then be a definite type of relation with one's fellow man," puts this position sharply.[12] The death-of-God theologies discussed above have this thrust. There is much of this emphasis in Dietrich Bonhoeffer's call for a "religionless Christianity," and it is easy to recognize the same theme in Henry Nelson Wieman's interpretation of God as "creative event," [13] and in Harvey Cox's "secular city." [14] But these are all explicitly theological authors; the search for the ultimate in the midst of human existence finds its most characteristic contemporary expression in the fact that it is shared by many who do not think of themselves as having or even seeking faith.

Thus on the one hand there is the quest for the distinctively religious, the quest for faith, the quest for the holy as such; and, on the other hand, there is the quest to identify oneself, whether a man of faith, or simply as a man, with men—the quest to be wholly a man. The expression of love we place in the second quest; it is a phase of faith in which faith is not conscious of itself. Yet love, as we understand it, is grounded in faith. As it is shown to us in the "model" of the New Testament, it is a turning away from oneself which can take place because one knows that he has been found, been

[12] Cf. the whole context of "The Problem of a New Testament Theology," in "The Bultmannian School of Biblical Interpretation: New Directions?" *The Journal for Theology and the Church* (New York: Harper Torchbooks, 1965), I, 167-83. Quotation from p. 183.

[13] Cf. H. N. Wieman, *The Source of Human Good* (Chicago: The University of Chicago Press, 1946).

[14] Harvey Cox, *The Secular City* (New York: The Macmillan Company, 1965).

accepted, by the "Thou" who is the foundation of his existence. The movement toward Christian action is thus a movement which springs from and is made possible by something
that is given, but the action itself moves toward being unconscious of itself and hence unconscious of what is given,
toward focusing wholly on understanding and being there
for the other. In its own understanding of itself, love finds
the "achievement orientation" transcended through what has
come to it in the receptive orientation, so that the action of
love does not intend to be achievement-oriented. That in fact
the acts which we think of as love do repeatedly, and often
unsuspectedly, re-express our achievement orientation is a
sign of the difficulty of recovery of faith and love.

The two lines of seeking which we have suggested above,
toward an authentic awareness of the Holy One and toward
an authentic identification with and acceptance of our fellowman, are in practice deeply interwoven.[15] Yet they continually
tend to fall apart, and the decay of religious forms has meant
that the second direction of searching has tended to have the
greater vitality. The religious quest must often be carried
forward in this very one-sided way, "in the absence of God,"
in our time. Honesty will require some to conceal from themselves the religious nature of their quest for true humanity
(strange as this may seem), because they will not be able
honestly to recognize any vitality in what is commonly known
as "religious." Others will recognize the basis of their quest
in faith, but will not be able to believe that this faith can

[15] Thus Bishop J. A. T. Robinson, who is best known for his book
Honest to God (Philadelphia: The Westminster Press, 1963) is also the
author of *Liturgy Coming to Life*. Cf. also George McLeod, *Only One Way
Left* (Glasgow: The Iona Community, 1956).

associate itself with any cultural form, including the existing religious forms. But it is our conviction that living, authentic humanity requires the dialectic of both searches—the quest for the Holy and the quest for the fellowman, the quest for faith and the quest for love.

HEROISM AS A PROBLEM

To clarify the dialectic of these two quests, it may be helpful to look at something that, at first sight, has little to do with them: the problem of heroism. For our time is particularly engrossed with the vision of the hero and of the heroic act, even though this preoccupation often appears in negative form as preoccupation with the "anti-hero." The kind of self-understanding that compels us to be preoccupied with the heroic sets the form within which we must grasp the meaning of faith and love.

On a popular level the hero is still a very positive figure. It is a striking disclosure of the nature of our "adolescent sub-culture" that school leaders who wanted to put greater stress on intellectual achievement have suggested several schemes by which to give the scholar some of the prestige of the popular adolescent hero, the athlete—as in the suggestion to award a "letter" to top scholars. One might hope that the thrust toward intellectual achievement would spring from a wider base than popular acclaim, but the suggestion at any rate is right in recognizing that both athlete and scholar are operating in the "achievement orientation" to which we referred above. Heroism in general is an intensification of this achievement orientation, or at least that is what we most readily see in it.

There is an ambiguity in our view of heroism, as to whether

we want to follow a hero or be one. But the hero is not out-grown as we leave adolescence, as an evening with television will quickly tell—provided one can assume that television is for post-adolescents. If we look into the area of public life, we see political figures presented to us as heroic figures, bigger than life size, protecting us from the monstrous evils that threaten us—an image that easily lends itself to demonic distortion. And in a very different way, James Thurber's figure, Walter Mitty, shows us that in our world even the most unheroic of men needs to see himself as a hero, even at the expense of losing contact with reality.

This preoccupation with the hero springs from our sense that a man's real self is disclosed in a situation that tests him to the utmost. We believe that we are not at our best until some great event brings forth, from a secret depth of our being, those resources which the daily round does not arouse. Hence the popular image of the hero presupposes that a man's environment, no matter how tragically it may crush his con-scious purpose, is nonetheless meaningfully related to his deepest self because it gives him the possibility of being a hero. The popular view also presupposes that, however twisted our nature is, and however inadequate our responses to "ordinary" life may be, men have in them (hopefully, we have in us) the potential of greatness or nobility: when the ultimate test comes, the hero emerges. From this standpoint the "limit situation" may be a failure as far as the concrete outcome is concerned, but the immediate failure will reveal the deeper greatness of man.

It is evident that this sort of self-understanding may be developed in varying degrees of depth and seriousness! But the artistically, or even ethically, superficial hero has something in common with the great tragic hero, and the serious grappling with life in our "heroic" legacy opens a way of understanding ourselves that all of us, to some degree, share. Further, while heroes are universal figures, and every culture has them, it seems that an almost obsessive involvement with the hero-image is characteristic of our Western individualistic self-consciousness. Partly, at least, this situation arises out of our Christian inheritance. For that tradition puts a singular emphasis on the individual self and its destiny. We may describe this intensification of self-awareness somewhat schematically by saying that the Christian view of man has given the self meaning by engrafting its momentary existence into a continuing lifetime of vocation in cumulative work in the service of God; and the continuing self of vocation has been given meaning by engrafting it into a divine history, a purposeful history which gives meaning and fulfillment to the otherwise fragile and temporary self.

In some other cultures the striving toward the heroic is understood in terms of meeting some temporary crisis, as is widely true in cultures based on the returning crisis of the seasons of the year. In these situations it may be possible to live out the expression of heroism, so to speak, and work it out of one's system. With us, on the other hand, the belief that our selves have deep and permanent meaning is profoundly ingrained—we are taught to feel that our selves have such significance that they must contribute—through vocation—to a lifetime of meaningful work, and beyond this will or at least ought to fit into a permanent and growing construction, the history to which we are contributing.

In understanding ourselves in this way, we have radically secularized the Christian understanding of faith, vocation, and history, and at the same time have so enclosed ourselves in the achievement-oriented side of our selfhood that the only way of breaking out often seems to be through the dream of heroic action, in which the achievement orientation is so intensified, by being pressed to the limits of human capacity, that it breaks out of itself and comes into contact with something beyond it. At the same time, though the popular imagination still has a very positive view of the hero (for instance, quite unreasonably expecting the hero to "save" us in political crises), the more thoughtful insight of our time has a remarkably ambiguous attitude toward the hero. The hero and the heroic are attractive and meaningful because we find ourselves compelled to explore ourselves by pitting ourselves—at least in imagination—against "limit situations" which test the total capacity of our being. But the hero and the heroic are distasteful and suspicious because we sense in them too easy a disposition of the problem of our preoccupation with ourselves. Furthermore, the decay of confidence in a meaningful environment has left the self, even when intensified to heroic proportions, desperately alone—related to nothing but itself and its own quest for freedom.

It is evident, too, that suspicion of a kind of false religious heroism lies at the heart of a good deal of the suspicion of the religious life that we have noticed. "Religious" activities are suspect in our time not merely because religion has become a function which is usually at the margin of the lives of those who profess it. More profoundly, "religious" activities are suspect because we feel them to be so deeply involved in our projections of ourselves. The interest in Eastern faith, to which we referred above, springs in good measure from a revulsion against the traditional Western way of finding meaning through self-expression and action. The attractiveness of this other tradition lies in the fact that in it, reality is found by a release from that drive to be a self which is so deeply embedded in the quest for heroic action.

THE SELF IN CHRISTIAN FAITH

The exaggerated sense of self which leads to our excessive preoccupation with ourselves is thus in good measure the fruit of a secularization of our religious heritage. For the sequence, "self-vocation-history," is an authentically Christian sequence, and in its intended meaning it interprets our life to us in terms of obedience and love as responses to the Holy God. But we in our culture have transposed this sequence of "self-vocation-history" into an expression of the self and its autonomous freedom. The result has been that this sequence of stages in understanding our selfhood has brought upon us an almost unbearable weight of self-consciousness.

In this situation it is not surprising that there is a widespread resentment against Christianity. Nor is it surprising that, to many, human love seems the only possible escape from the prison of the self. The quest for love is not the only form which the quest for an ultimate reality may take, but it is the most widespread and significant form in which we see the search for the ultimate going on around us. As Archibald MacLeish puts it:

> Blow on the coal of the heart . . .
> The lights have gone out in the sky.[16]

We have touched above on the many-sided meaning of

[16] *J.B.* (Boston: Houghton Mifflin Company, 1958), p. 153. Reprinted by permission.

"love." Here we note only two things: that the self-giving and openness of generous love come in deeply interwoven combinations with possessiveness and the drive for self-fulfillment; and that the modern imagination, which seizes on the movement of self-giving as the vision of the ultimate which animates the frustrated grasping of possessive forms of love, is often quite unable to see the acceptance and sustaining by the Holy One which Christian faith knows to be the ground of generous love.

The Christian does not stand apart from the realities of his time. The secularism of our time does not mean that the church is surrounded by a secular world, so that it fights off a surrounding sea of secularism—though this way of thinking is widely prevalent in the churches. It is far more honest to say that God is distant from the churches, just as he is distant from the culture at large. It may even be that he is often more distant from the consciously religious people, whose form of religion so easily becomes a shield to protect them from the uncompromising claims of God. In other words, the reality of the presence of God is a reality which escapes the consciously religious person quite as readily as it does the consciously secular person. In the actual place where they live, religious people, too, normally begin their search for the ultimate with a search for human love, though they may use a somewhat different vocabulary from what they would find in some contemporary novels. And for religious people, the undergirding, accepting act of God constantly tends to become unreal. The Christian cannot stand off and judge the "faithless love" (i.e., love that is not explicitly grounded in faith) which he sees around him, for he must acknowledge that he lives in much the same way, even though his eyes are open to another way of being grasped by love, a possibility which he affirms is realized for him in moments of faith and decision.

We may gain a clearer view of how Christian faith may speak to this situation if we let it address the secularized distortion of faith which was mentioned above: the framework in which the momentary self finds security in a lifetime of vocation, and the achievement of vocation, in turn, contributes to an overarching and growing historical pattern.

FAITH AS JUDGMENT

First we note that the secular version of history as a continuing process which meaningfully absorbs the deposit of our life-work is sharply opposed by the judgment of Christian faith. In faith, history is seen as a burden from which one can be set free only by death—by dying to the purpose of projecting one's life into future history. Faith does not promise this sort of continuity to men. Quite the opposite, it closes off this sort of hope to the self which confronts it. The greatness of a nation, or of a culture, or of a type of scientific achievement—these are not enduring realities. Whether it is harder for this judgment to be heard by those who have power and are afraid of losing it, or by those who have been dispossessed in our world and are struggling for recognition, is not easy to say. But there can be no doubt that the uncompromising word of Christian faith to both groups is: there is no ultimate security or fulfillment in history, in the continuing flow of man's empirical historical existence.

Further, Christian faith does not even promise a continuous life of meaningful vocation. The notion that a man or woman can hope to see the expected results of a generation of faithful, moral work is widely held to be a Christian idea—for instance in the interpretation of the work of parents for their children. But in Christian faith there is no promise that things will turn out this way. One is called upon to create conditions of freedom, and to expose the new generation to the hard realities of life. One acts in faith that there is a God, known in Christ, and that one's wisdom and love, such as they are, may do something to make it possible for him to speak to the new generation. But rather than thinking of parenthood in the protective pattern which is common, we would do well to understand that even to this stage of our selfhood, where we try to understand ourselves as fitting into a lifetime or generation of work, Christian faith makes no promise about how things will come out. Here again, it is by accepting the death of our claim to our own projection of our selves in a lifetime of work that we find the freedom of faith—and the illustration of vocation chosen (parenthood) should help to show that the death of this projection of self may clear the way for a kind of love that is open to the son or daughter as the protective kind cannot be.

The illustration of the vocation of being a parent is in one way too easy. For whatever its tragedies and failures, parent-hood is a vocation which explicitly has room for confronting a "thou." It is hard to find the connection between this basic springing-point of Christian action and many other vocations. Here we shall not try to enter into this problem except to make the same negative point: Christian faith pulls the foundation out from any hope that a life can find ultimate security in vocation. Whatever one's devotion to vocation may be, it is sharply relativized by faith: here we have no enduring achievements.

In the same way, pressing to the final point in the series, faith does not allow the self to be secure in its moment of decision. Here, too, the first word of faith is the word of judgment: you are not sufficient for this moment. Of the many ways in which the "no" of faith is spoken to man in his quest for a place for himself, none is clearer than the most familiar —the impact of the Sermon on the Mount upon the serious reader. "Whoever is angry with his brother is in danger of the judgment. . . . Turn the other cheek. . . . Love your enemies and pray for your persecutors. . . . Do not be anxious for tomorrow. . . . Be perfect as your father in heaven is perfect." Well known as they are, these sayings have not lost their bite. They speak of our freedom to confront the "other," and they take this freedom with the utmost seriousness. At the same time, no honest reader can think of these sayings without hearing them speak to him of his insufficiency. They are tragically misunderstood if they are taken simply as calling for an effort, and for a repression of negative tendencies. They call for a radical transformation, a radical restructuring of the self, and they do so in the context of a faith that the moment of transformation is at hand, impinging upon life.

FAITH AS ROOTAGE

The message of faith is a message of acceptance. But this side of faith's meaning can be heard only by passing through the hearing of its opposite, the "no" to life as we project it. In its initial confrontation with our achievement orientation, Christian faith speaks traditionally of judgment and death, a judgment and death of precisely those projections of the self, in its achievement orientation, into the moment of decision, into vocation, and into history. Only he who is able to listen to this negative word is able to respond in faith and hear the serious promise of faith. Yet it is also true that the strong sense of self, which is expressed in our pronounced achievement orientation and in our involvement with the vision of heroism, does spring from a distortion of the authentic Christian sequence of self-vocation-history within the context of faith. Can the authentic Christian sequence still be seen and lived in, despite the fact that all of us are pervaded by a different meaning of this sequence? We believe that it can, and we would look for its meaning in the following direction.

The Christian faith does not rest in the receptive orientation, but has deeply built into it a dialectic or alternation between the receptive orientation and an active orientation, which we may call a "transfigured achievement orientation." Worship, the encounter with God, takes place in receptivity, in being open, often in the sense of a negation or choking-off of the achievement-understanding of the self. But worship is understood as participation in an action in which the achievement orientation is transcended, and Christian faith does not leave the self permanently in the situation where it has stopped, silenced itself, and thereby been enabled for something to "come" to it.

God's love, then, has as its first word a word that is not unique to itself. You do not have to have faith to know that men die and that their achievements come to nothing. But this word of honest acceptance of the transiency of life and the inability of the self to find a place in which it can stand securely is a genuine word of love. In hearing it—for the Christian, in and through the event of Christ—one is able to hear that he is accepted and supported in the purpose of God. "In the purpose of God"—this means that the self is drawn into action, into a "transfigured achievement orientation," in which are joined the moment of being there for the

125

other, the continuing purpose of giving to the other as a continuing being, and the participation in the "history" of God's purpose.[17]

That in fact this new orientation does not endure in our existence—that it has to be renewed in responsible decision —and that even in a moment of decision it does not appear in a pure state but shows itself in action mixed with the simple achievement orientation, does not nullify the reality of the new, nor the possibility that it can make a difference in actual decisions. The fact that these decisions tend to be erased and absorbed by the flow of events which spring from other sources, and that they do appear in mixtures of which we are often unaware, forcefully indicates that faith calls for a total transformation of life, a transformation hinted at by the love which is possible to all men. This is the promise of faith: not that the self which we project into the future shall endure, but that love, now known as a fragment or a possibility, shall come to be the reality.

We may sum it up by quoting Bultmann's interpretation of the meaning of faith for Jesus:

Faith is for him the power, in particular moments of life, to take seriously the conviction of the omnipotence of God; it is the certainty that in such particular moments God's activity is really experienced; it is the conviction that the distant God is really the God near at hand, if man will only relinquish his usual attitude and be ready to see the nearness of God. In the sense of

[17] For an attempt to show how in one part of the New Testament it is believed that the active self may be taken up into a "transfigured achievement orientation," cf. William A. Beardslee, *Human Achievement and Divine Vocation in the Message of Paul* (Naperville, Ill.: Alec R. Allenson, 1961).

Jesus it is possible to have faith only if one is obedient, and thus every frivolous misuse of faith in God is excluded.[18]

At this point let us take a new problem and turn our attention from the response of the self to Christian faith to the response of the self in simple openness to the other. There is a striking similarity. Here again, the achievement orientation of the self is stopped by awareness of the other, and something may "come" creatively to the self made receptive by confronting the other—"come" not just in the sense of reciprocity or the fulfillment of longing, but in the deeper sense of the opening of a new level of reality, the awareness of something more to life than the line along which I project myself. Here, too, we find the same dialectic between passive and active, and the self comes from an encounter with an other with a "transfigured achievement orientation," an openness and intention of putting the resources of his life at the disposal of the other.

As an illustration, consider a very common experience, a crisis in the relation between two persons. One of the partners in a marriage must have a very serious operation. This is primarily a crisis to the one who is sick, and we run the risk of appearing as comical as the fathers in the maternity section if we look at such a crisis from the other side. It is nonetheless more useful for our purpose to look at it from the point of view of the one who is in a sense a spectator in a struggle of life and death. Whatever the outcome of the operation, such an experience often opens one's eyes anew to the presence of the other person, to the meaning and possibilities of the marriage, and to what has been given to him in it. The inter-

[18] *Jesus and the Word,* trans. Louise P. Smith and Erminie Huntress (New York: Charles Scribner's Sons, 1934), pp. 190-91.

play of passive and active is well shown by this sort of experience, for the primacy of the receptive orientation is clear: one becomes freshly aware of this personal relationship by coming into a situation in which he is not able to do anything directly. But the active orientation, the "transfigured achievement orientation," is also integral; such a new realization of the gift of life would be meaningless if it did not issue into action. This illustration also makes clear that, while action is inevitable, the deep experience itself does not directly prescribe any specific action. Such a realization of awakening carries with it the responsibility of working out the appropriate action as well as one can. An experience of this sort is also to the point because in it life is received as a precarious and fragile gift, not as a permanent possession. Yet, the awareness of the temporariness of the gift of life does not detach one from his commitment to the marriage; on the contrary, it can deepen it and make it more tough and resilient. At the same time such a moment of awareness by no means converts the relationship into an "ideal" one. It can make possible, within the actual sociological and personal structure of the marriage, some acts which bring to expression a self not centered on itself. This manner of being pushed to one's limit within the daily and "humdrum" relationships of life thus compels a more radical transformation than the escapist "heroic" imagination which we so easily substitute for it.

One could easily brush aside this model of love because it is so easily sentimentalized. Yet, it is in just such simple, yet deep, experiences that we must look for a model to give meaning to relationships which are not nearly so direct.

Turning at last to our initial question: does love need to be understood as a religious act? the answer will be: it does not "need" to in the sense that it does not logically demand this. In another sense the "need" of love for the supportive base of faith is clear enough. It can get along without this, and its need is no justification for giving it this support. In fact, faith confronts *this* need with a "no," with the death of the longing for fulfillment, as noted above. But love does need to be interpreted as a religious act within the context of Christian faith. Within that context, the structural similarity between the confrontation of the self by God in Christ and the confrontation of the self by the other can be seen to have its meaning in the relation between faith and love. Within that context, the incompleteness of love is not rationally rounded out, but it is sustained by the faith that the fragmentary motions of love, transient and imperfect as they always are, will be taken up into the purpose of God and find their fulfillment. From the context of faith, love needs to be understood as a religious act.

The analysis of love and faith shows that the understanding of love as the expression and outcome of faith can be sustained only if the life of faith is sustained, and thus points to the urgency of a clearer grasp of the meaning of faith in relation to the world. To this question of faith and the world we now turn.

V
In the World but Not of the World

The Christian is the most worldly of all persons, subject to the ambiguity and finiteness of human life, and knowing that fulfillment of his life comes through the world.

The Christian is the most unworldly of all persons, released from ultimate concern about any event within the finiteness and conditionedness of human life, and knowing that the fulfillment of his life does not come from the world.

Many ideas expressed in this book depend for their actual meaning upon the interpretation given to the expression that the Christian is "in the world but not of it."

A clever quipster has seen through this way of understanding the life of the Christian today, and has reversed the statement to the effect that a Christian is one who is "*of* the world but not *in* it." The quipster's version has a sting to it precisely because of the inadequacy of the popular version. The popular version *"in* the world but not *of* it" describes what the Christian thinks he ought to be. The quipster's version, *"of* the world but not *in* it," unfortunately, in far too many instances, describes what the Christian *is.*

One of the questions which many people have raised about Bishop Robinson's provocative book, *Honest to God,* concerns his failure to make a clear distinction between God and the world. Particularly in the instances of "prayer" and the "new morality" as well as in the idea of "worldly holiness," the Bishop seems to have dissolved the difference between God and the world in favor of the world, leaving no content in the language or the idea of God. These questions are aggravated by Bonhoeffer's references to the "world come of age" and to the fact that now that the world has come of age, it is more godless than ever, and perhaps nearer to God than ever before. Let us use the question about Bishop Robinson and Dietrich Bonhoeffer as a way of picking up a reference to the world from chapter II and testing its adequacy to our present situation.

At a particular point in the discussion above, we spoke of the meaning of "world."

"World" is in fact not a category of objective reality, so that there are certain objective, definable things that are always "world," or certain acts or desires that are always wrong because worldly. "World" is rather a name for those structures or patterns in which we encapsule ourselves, shelter ourselves from the claim of faith and love, and it is only insofar as we do this that the term can be applied.[1]

[1] Chapter III, p. 96.

While holding to the main thesis here, we must go further, for both Robinson and Bonhoeffer speak of a "worldly holiness" which this definition of world would not allow.

In the Protestant tradition pietism has given the prevailing definition to "world" as objective evil and it is against the background of pietism that the phrase, "in the world but not of it," is commonly understood. The implication is that "world" is the sphere of evil powers, and, derivatively, that certain actions or passions are evil and to be avoided. The distinction between sacred and secular callings, the Holy and the profane, moral and immoral actions, blessing and cursing, important in the quality of awareness it illuminates, leads to an error if the distinction is applied spatially. The community of the righteous (church or otherwise) tends to recognize no evil in itself and no good in the community outside itself. Certain activities are always evil, "politics," for example. The Sabbath or Sunday is set apart as a "holy day" and certain religious activities such as worship, meditation, or reading are "proper" to the day, over against such secular activities as labor, business, or commerce.

Sex is another activity that tends to be regarded as evil, and so thoroughly disapproved by the religious community that a criterion of sexual normalcy becomes problematic. If all heterosexual desire and activity are evil, it is no wonder that many in our culture come to think of homosexual acts as less "sexual," less risky perhaps, and certainly less evil. On the other hand vast numbers of persons fall for a sort of sensational, exteriorized, publicized sexuality in which there is eroticism but no love, because they have never been able to understand the propriety and pleasure of sexual fulfillment within love. Waldo Beach's quip about Christian marriage being a "sexless communion between two pale saints" [2] is to the point. But we disagree.

In the definition of world above, we are rejecting the "spatial" understanding within which certain things or acts are always "world" or "worldly" and wrong because worldly. Whatever is wrong is not wrong because it is worldly but because it violates the meaning of love and human fulfillment. Because the only unambiguous Christian virtue is love and the only surd evil the failure to love, it is impossible to "locate" wrong in a space in creation or confine it to an elemental characteristic of human nature. All qualities of human creativity are legitimized in God's judgment upon the creation as "good," and his declaring all foods clean (Acts 10:9-16). It remains true that every ability may indeed be misused in such a way as to create evil. But this is a matter of history and time, a matter of the particular uses of power, and not an inevitable quality of the power or ability itself. The misuse is not necessary to the function. To designate the function itself as evil is to spatialize man's life, marking off certain areas or certain abilities as themselves evil. It is clear, then, that we do not allow flesh or sex or appetite or "places" to be seen as worldly and consequently evil.

With this in mind, however, we are not finished with the problem. The definition previously given also asserts that "world" is those structures and patterns which we create and participate in, closing ourselves off thereby from the claims of the Holy upon us, to the claims of faith and love. World is a kind of shell or womb within which we agree to recognize by a process of self-deception only questions we ask or have

<hr>

[2] *Conscience on Campus* (New York: Association Press, 1958), p. 92.

interest in. We pretend to live without an ultimate dimension, saying "yes" so completely to horizontal concerns and achievements that we, in effect, bracket out the transcendent. We define humanness in ever more manageable, but ever more restricted, terms, insisting inordinately upon our creation of ourselves to the neglect of the presence of Mystery or Grace. We are, in effect, what we think we are, what we take ourselves to be, and we are, in fact, pretty flat people; for we are unable to accept ourselves as God takes us to be. We are lost both to the possibility of being guilty and of being forgiven.

Bonhoeffer and Robinson, in speaking of "holy worldliness" and "the world come of age," seem to be out of step if they are asking us to "encapsule" ourselves against faith and love. There is a subtlety to their analysis, however, and one may be assured that they are not calling him to the bland life of modern technological man in the name of Christ. Actually there are two moves here. The first is to recognize that "world" is not concentrated evil, the second is to recognize that church or Holy is not concentrated goodness. To turn the figures, the first is to recognize the inadequacy of identifying good or evil with objective structures, the second is to recognize the nebulousness of good or evil without objective structures. At one point in our cultural history it was important that we be called from contacts with "world" which would encapsule us against Christ. In our own day Bonhoeffer and Robinson call us to recognize that man can also "encapsule" himself against God's demands by refusing to participate in the world.

Thus it was necessary in chapter III for us to say more about "world" than we did immediately above. We had to speak of a re-engagement with the world, as love spends itself in affirming another person.

We see that the openness of love requires a double movement toward those environing and inward structures which we call "the world": a movement of detachment from them, in faith, as one disengages himself from "the world" and a re-engagement in the world in love, as one acts with what understanding he can muster in the encounter with the "other," to affirm the other's life in the actual situation he is in.[3]

Protestantism of the first half of the twentieth century would have agreed theoretically with the nonspatial definition of world, yet, in practice, it fostered a romantic attitude toward Jesus as Christ, denying Jesus' manhood, and it promoted a religious individualism which offered personal salvation, a salvation "from" the world. The understanding of sacredness suggested by this romantic individualism was effeminate and cautious, God never really coming into contact with the hard brutalities of man's common life. The social-political gospel of Rauschenbusch and Reinhold Niebuhr encountered rough going among a people whose concept of individual religious fulfillment is suggested by the popular hymn:

> Into my heart, into my heart.
> Come into my heart, Lord Jesus;
> Come in today, come in to stay,
> Come into my heart, Lord Jesus.

Even in the case of Bonhoeffer it was only after intense struggle that he could bring himself to break the identifica-

[3] Chapter III, p. 98.

tion with "Jesus-type" actions and participate in and encourage those who were seeking to kill Hitler in order to save thousands of lives.[4]

The revolt of Bonhoeffer (and Robinson and Tillich, as well) is not really against a "world" or a "religion" in which man encapsules himself against God's demands but against an effeminate inward and spiritual pietism which emasculates faith by separating it from the blood and flesh, danger and courage, suffering and compromise, of the worldly situation. The cultural ground has shifted rather radically since the first century. At that time "world" indicated a "realm" or "eon" within which man could hide from God's eschatological claim. In the twentieth century, the Christian is called to acknowledge Christ's presence where it is, that is, in the "world," over against a spiritualized, sentimental, personal, and individual piety within which man secures himself against the real demands of God's righteousness.

Perhaps the lesson of our history is that all action involves structure, and that man is capable of building a defense against the claims of God either through the structures of public life *or* through the vain imagining of righteousness in one's own heart. Bonhoeffer found German Protestantism to be naïve in its nurture of individual faith in God to the neglect of God's demand of justice in the public orders of life. Robinson found post World War II English Christianity to be meticulous in personal moral niceties to the neglect of the one inescapable commandment that man love his neighbor. No one questions the sincerity or the good intentions of the people

[4] See Elizabeth Berryhill, *The Cup of Trembling* (New York: Seabury Press, n.d.) a one-act play upon the theme of Bonhoeffer's struggle between piety without guilt and faith with guilt.

Bonhoeffer and Robinson are criticizing. But their bias against the fleshliness and sordidness of the world made it impossible for them to be realistic in helping their neighbors in the hour of crisis.

It is within this kind of cultural situation that Bonhoeffer appeals, not against the world, but for a "worldly holiness." Let us consider his position more closely. For if Bonhoeffer is right, we may be forced to a transformation of our understanding of the life of the Christian and of the life of the church in our day.

LIFE IN THE WORLD

Some of the most stimulating utterances, even if fragmentary and puzzling, to come out of the Second World War years are those of Dietrich Bonhoeffer. The meaning which Bonhoeffer gives to the world is the same as that quoted above, but he emphasizes the role of autonomous man in creating a cultural situation, the world. Indeed, the experience of man since the Renaissance and the Industrial Revolution has been to exercise an increasing degree of creativity so that man's present world is more obviously man's creation than it is God's. Religion resisted man's creative thrust, emphasizing submission to God in passivity rather than presumptuous activity by man. No human act of itself is worth the possibility of arousing God's wrath. So went the reasoning! If one takes a further step he will maintain that one ought to know that an act meets God's approval before it is committed. The force of religion was conservative, restricting both man's imagination and his creativity.

Renaissance man collapsed this picture by affirming his autonomy through an increasing release of all his capacities toward the understanding, the fashioning, even the mastering of his fate. Man's elemental and unquestioning dependence upon God became an elemental and questioning dependence upon one's own effort to make something better of his world and of his life. Within this change in orientation religion fell into retreat, clinging to those areas of man's life over which man had not yet gained control, the "gaps" and "missing links" about which science had not yet spoken. Bonhoeffer refers to this attitude toward God as toward a *deus ex machina* whose actual effect upon human life would inevitably diminish with every quantitative expansion of man's own powers.

Confronted with this strange defensive role by religion to hold some ground for the sake of God, Bonhoeffer turns the table and welcomes the present world as "come of age" and perhaps closer to God than ever before.

At the same time that Bonhoeffer was reassessing the significance of man's creative effort, Luther's idea that man is simultaneously sinful and forgiven (*simul peccator et iustus*) was receiving fresh attention. In both instances the quantitative relationship between God's action and man's is rejected in favor of a more dynamic, dialectical, and qualitative relationship between them. It is thus possible to see man's action not necessarily as a rebellion against God, but as an inevitable assertion of oneself if he is to be a man. More about this later. At the moment it is enough to say that the "world come of age" does not necessarily mean a world set against God, but a world in which man, come of age, accepts the challenge to be a man, to create, to exercise freedom and responsibility, to become guilty, to risk guilt in order to open the possibility of a genuine human fulfillment.

As regards the particular topic at hand, the effect of

Bonhoeffer's position is to reverse the meaning of world as a "capsule" in which man denies God's claim, maintaining that it is precisely in this world come of age, this world of man's creativity, that God has acted. This means that one cannot flee from the evil world in order to be with God, nor can he draw a line through the world separating the evil from the good. God is present in the world, loving the world and everything in it, working to cleanse, reconcile, renew, redeem, and fulfill; working to bring the created, temporal, and spatial world to that for which it was made. God and the religious concern, then, have to do not with a special realm in history or a special super-temporal or post-temporal existence, but with a dimension of everything that now is. Consequently the effect of religion is to affirm the world and one's existence in the world *in a particular way.* Man's creative self-expression and self-realization are not condemned but encouraged. Instead of cultivating an attitude of depreciation toward the world and detachment from it, Christianity calls one to a life of creativity within the world through the exercise of faith, opposing only that "worldliness" which is indifferent to the transcendent or degrading to man. With Bonhoeffer, then, the case for religion rests upon one's affirmation of God's act in "the center of the village." Whether we like it or not, God himself has chosen to be present in the center of this ambiguous world, sending rain upon the just and unjust, comprehending the full spectrum of good and evil, seeking the healing and redirection of evil and not just promoting the triumph of good over evil. God is in the world acting to create a community of faith, hope, and love, not a community of "other-worldly" or "good" people. Christ is present in the world, and the Christian is called to observe that presence by being in the world.

The New Testament passages which inform Bonhoeffer's position are the incarnational passages in John, the atonement passages in Paul, and the Gospel passages of Jesus' proclamation.

In the prologue to the Fourth Gospel, the writer makes two drastic claims, the second of which is: "And the Word became flesh and dwelt among us, full of grace and truth" (John 1:14a). With Bonhoeffer the emphasis of this passage is thoroughly incarnational. Whether men accept God's presence in fleshly existence is not nearly as important as the fact that God is present in the flesh of the world. In Christ God has chosen to be in the world, suffering with and for the world, and effecting a hallowing of all worldly existence *in* history rather than saving a few people *out* of history. For Bonhoeffer this is the critical difference between Christianity and religion or religions. In his words, "This is the decisive difference between Christianity and all religions. Man's religiosity makes him look in his distress to the power of God in the world; he uses God as a *Deus ex machina*. The Bible, however, directs him to the powerlessness and suffering of God; only a suffering God can help." [5]

According to this view, God is present not only in what others call good, but also in what they call evil. For this reason one is not to root up everything that seems to be evil.[6] God

---

[5] Letter, July 16, 1944, in *Letters and Papers from Prison* (London: SCM Press, 1953; trans. of the German original *Widerstand und Ergebung* [München: Chr. Kaiser Verlag, 1952]; publ. by Macmillan as *Prisoner for God* [New York: The Macmillan Company, 1953], and as *Letters and Papers from Prison* [Macmillan Paperbacks Edition, 1962]).

[6] Cf. parable of the weeds (wheat and tares), Matt. 13:24-30.

is drawn into the evil as well as into the goodness of the flesh. Helmut Thielicke stands with Bonhoeffer when he suggests that we cannot draw Christ too deeply into the flesh. With the same interpretation Robert McAfee Brown writes: "Our theology does not separate us from the world. It ties us more closely to it," [7] and W. H. Auden finishes his "Christmas Oratorio":

> He is the Life
> Love Him in the World of the Flesh:
> And at your marriage all its occasions
> shall dance for joy.

Bonhoeffer's way of putting it is to say that Jesus claims for himself and the kingdom of God the whole of human life in all its manifestations.[8]

Bonhoeffer is influenced to take a position "in the world" also by the atonement passages of Paul, especially II Corinthians 5:19: "God was in Christ reconciling the world to himself, not counting their trespasses against them, and entrusting to us the message of reconciliation." Without question Bonhoeffer was repelled by a cautious and timid approach to the world which suggested that Christ was in the church but Satan was in the world. He was also incensed by a paternalistic interpretation of the Christian life which causes one to live in fear that he will lose Christ in the world. With the possible overexuberance of a warrior he claims God's action not just to help us when our powers are used up, not just to keep us from evil, not just in our weakness, but in the very center of the village of our finite and fleshly life, with partial

[7] "Theology as an Act of Gratitude," *Union Seminary Quarterly Review,* December, 1960, p. 93.
[8] Letter, June 20, 1944.

control of our destiny *and* fear before our destiny, with good *and* evil so intertwined that they can never be completely separated, with weakness *and* strength.[9] For Bonhoeffer, then, the life of the Christian is altogether in this present ambiguous time and place, this world, for it is precisely here that God has chosen to enflesh himself, to act and to be present for the healing of mankind.[10] Because Christ is in the world, that is where the Christian is, identifying himself with what Paul calls God's reconciliation of the world, and striving to be a man, participating "in the suffering of God in the life of the world." [11]

What possible meaning could *"in* the world but not *of* it" have within Bonhoeffer's interpretation of Christian faith and the world? No meaning at all, without qualification of the terms and the addition of other terms. The life of a Christian in a "world come of age" is, against pietism and "spirituality," a life *in* the world and a life *of* the world. But it is the world understood in a particular way and affirmed with a peculiarly religious quality of conviction and action. This position is so radically different from traditional thought about the meaning of the life of the individual Christian and the nature of the church that separate consideration must be given to it.

[9] "We must not wait until we are at the end of our tether: he [God] must be found at the centre of life: in life, and not only in death; in health and vigour, and not only in suffering; in activity, and not only in sin. The ground for this lies in the revelation of God in Christ. Christ is the centre of life, and in no sense did he come to answer our unsolved problems. From the centre of life certain questions are seen to be wholly irrelevant, and so are the answers commonly given to them—I am thinking for example of the judgement pronounced on the friends of Job. In Christ there are no Christian problems." (Letter, May 25, 1944.)
[10] Cf. Phil. 2:7-8 and Col. 1:19-20, NEB.
[11] Letter, July 18, 1944.

THE TRANSFORMATION OF PERSPECTIVE

Every piece of writing reflects to some extent the culture within which it is conceived and from which it emerges. The traces of the culture are evident in the mood, style, vocabulary, and ideas of the writing. This is true for every book, even the Bible, although the cultural or "time bound" dimension may be considerably less extensive and important in one work than in another. The writing of Dietrich Bonhoeffer is no exception to the rule, and it would not be unusual if much of what he wrote in a Nazi prison awaiting execution were influenced by the particular distress of his situation.[12] Contrary to what might be expected, however, Bonhoeffer's forced spatial separation from the world of nature and history becomes the occasion for a fresh and vigorous affirmation of the creation, of the world of the flesh. He does not welcome death as a release from his personal pain, nor does he gladly surrender this world in the imminent expectation of another and better heavenly world. Rather, he holds to the vitalities and meanings of this present life all the more tightly. Death is an awesome reality because of its threat to the meaning of life *in this world*. It was in this mood that Bonhoeffer wrote: "It is only when one loves life and the world so much that without them everything would be gone, that one can believe in the resurrection and a new world." [13]

One is not to pass over this world any longer in favor of the next, but to affirm the presence of a "Beyond in the midst

[12] For an account of Bonhoeffer's struggle with the Third Reich and of his incarceration and execution, see the introduction by John W. Doberstein to Bonhoeffer's *Life Together* (New York: Harper & Row, 1954) and E. Bethge's foreword to Bonhoeffer's *Letters and Papers from Prison.*

[13] Letter, Advent II, 1943.

of the world," "the Holy in the common." [14] Previously the figure of the pilgrim passing through this world to a better one beyond was formative for one's understanding of Christian existence. There is a soundness and authenticity to this view whether it is appropriated in the straight biblical text, "On this earth we have no continuing home but seek one to come," [15] or in the compelling musical setting of the text which Brahms has accomplished in the *Deutsches Requiem.* If the "pilgrim" or "sojourner" motif is developed to the point of denial of the world, however, a sharp conflict arises with the claim of God's "incarnation." [16] What has authenticity in the pilgrim image is that there is no permanence in the world. This is as true for Bonhoeffer as for another, for Bonhoeffer has absorbed this insight into his own position.

What has happened in the history of culture and religion is that the legitimate function of the pilgrim image has been extended to cover the entire meaning of Christian life, with the result that the world is fully overstepped and the Christian is understood as living completely in terms of a hope for a future heaven with no "presence" of God or the Holy in the "now." Dietrich Bonhoeffer and Gerhard Ebeling have exposed this development more clearly than others, and their work may be understood as a counter-thrust to an exclusive

[14] Cf. Robinson, *Honest to God* (Philadelphia: The Westminster Press, 1963), chaps. 3 and 5.

[15] Heb. 13:14, King James Version. A comparison with the Revised Standard Version and the New English Bible is interesting. "For here we have no lasting city, but we seek the city that is to come" (RSV). "For here we have no permanent home, but we are seekers after the city which is to come" (NEB).

[16] For an impressive positive use of the pilgrim image, see Gabriel Marcel, *Homo Viator* (Chicago: Henry Regnery Company, 1951).

other-worldliness.[17] It is possible that the counter-thrust may be so intemperate as to be an exclusive "worldliness." A judgment on this question is not as important at the moment, however, as the recognition of the transformation of perspective that has taken place.

Bonhoeffer's most brief and crisp utterance on the point is in the poem "Christians and Unbelievers."

> Men go to God when they are sore bestead,
> Pray to him for succour, for his peace, for bread,
> For mercy for them sick, sinning or dead:
> All men do so, Christian and unbelieving.

> Men go to God when he is sore bestead,
> Find him poor and scorned, without shelter or bread,
> Whelmed under weight of the wicked, the weak, the dead:
> Christians stand by God in his hour of grieving.

> God goeth to every man when sore bestead,
> Feedeth body and spirit with his bread,
> For Christians, heathens alike he hangeth dead:
> And both alike forgiving.[18]

Bonhoeffer does not negate stanzas one and two in the climactic third stanza, but he quite clearly indicates that one has not gotten to the center of the issue of Christian faith until one gets to and through stanza three. The effect of God's reality in the first stanza is to be a power to which man can turn for succor, peace, bread. The parable of the prodigal son also says much about the nature of the Father to maintain an attitude of concern, of helpfulness, and of compassion

---

[17] See Gerhard Ebeling's lectures at the University of Zürich, *The Nature of Faith* (*Das Wesen des christlichen Glaubens*), trans. R. G. Smith (London: Collins, 1959).

[18] In *Letters and Papers from Prison,* Macmillan Paperbacks Edition, pp. 224-25.

toward the son even though the son does not care for the Father until he gets into a situation he cannot handle within his resources.

In the second stanza, Bonhoeffer speaks of God's "emptying himself" and accepting responsibility for the hungry, wicked, and weak, God's presence among men to suffer with and for them. The Christian at this point is asked to affirm the suffering of God (perhaps only a temporary suffering) and through watchfulness to accept and participate in the passion of Christ.

In both these instances it is possible to interpret God's Christly action in terms of a "redeemer" who saves one out of the distress of the world, out of a life of hunger, war, evil, and sin. But the third stanza declares unambiguously God's presence *in* the world and *for* the world, for Christians and heathens alike. God's presence as a Beyond in our midst to give bread and forgiveness to body and spirit becomes pivotal in the transformation of perspective. A "presence" is celebrated here and now, not just preparing one for eternity, but blessing, healing, and fulfilling the present world. God is not "used" as relief from emergency. He is acknowledged within the emergency, and he is acknowledged there not in order to escape the emergency, but as a "presence" with one in and through the emergency. Man's quest for God as the "highest Good" or as the "Ultimate" or as a "Power for successful living," a quest largely prompted by God's absence, is confronted with the claim that God is present in the situation suffering with man, offering him a new understanding of himself born out of God's love for him but in complete respect for man's freedom, a claim prompted by the presence of the

Holy. It is not necessary in either case to say that God is completely absent or present, but it is important to recognize the radical difference between these forms of understanding. And, again, it is not only that the change is a change in direction from man's going to God to God's coming to man. What is most significant about the change is the qualitative difference there is in the nature of God. God takes the initiative in Bonhoeffer's view, and this initiative is taken unconditionally, whether man's whim or disposition or emergency inclines him to seek God or not. Further, God is present not to "save" persons out of the world or from the evil of the world, but to "save" them in the world, with whatever degrees of good or evil one might regard the world to have. Instead of God's being the last questionable being, dependent in some way upon man's search or need for him, God becomes the first unquestionable presence in such a way that all of man's inclinations and disinclinations, successes and failures, good and evil actions, transpire within this presence. Instead of God's questionable, problematic presence in an emergency, he is an inescapable presence in the ordinary, yet "present" in such a way that at times he seems to be absent or indifferent.

This view has serious and fascinating implications for the life of the individual Christian and for the life of the church. Governing the interpretation in both instances is a segment of Paul's letter to the Corinthians.

From now on, therefore, we regard no one from a human point of view; even though we once regarded Christ from a human point of view, we regard him thus no longer. Therefore, if any one is in Christ, he is a new creation; the old has passed away, behold, the new has come. All this is from God, who through

Christ reconciled us to himself and gave us the ministry of reconciliation; that is, God was in Christ reconciling the world to himself, not counting their trespasses against them, and entrusting to us the message of reconciliation. So we are ambassadors for Christ, God making his appeal through us . . . . Our mouth is open to you, Corinthians; our heart is wide. You are not restricted by us, but you are restricted in your own affections. In return—I speak as to children—widen your hearts also. (II Cor. 5:16-20; 6:11-13.)

IMPLICATIONS FOR THE LIFE OF
THE INDIVIDUAL CHRISTIAN

For many persons the shift of emphasis represented by the transformation under discussion has occurred within the context of a revolutionary discovery of the grace of God. Both terms are important in the expression, both *grace* and *God*. The quality of grace is unconditional gift (forgiveness, love), but it is the grace of *God,* of the only one about whom man is ultimately concerned.

Most of our discussion of religion places an ultimate sanction upon correct ideas or correct actions or proper social relations. Consequently, to question the particular idea of God is to be an atheist, to do an "unchristian act" is to be a non-Christian, to question the identity of a social pattern with the kingdom of God (segregation or integration, free enterprise system or socialism) is to place oneself outside that Kingdom. In each of these cases "being a Christian" is a matter primarily contingent upon what man thinks or does. God is, as it were, beyond him, uttering a "thou shalt" to man, and accepting man only when he obeys. The critical issue in one's Christian existence is not God's establishment of man's whole being, not God's act in man's behalf, but the partial act of man (feeling, willing, thinking, or acting—no one of which is ever a full expression of one's being) in relation to the Divine. Here the perspective is tied too closely with an element within the perspective, the function of faith reduced to the function of an aspect or part of man.

The transformation under discussion does not fall into the category of such an adjustment of understanding, expressions, beliefs, or actions within an uncriticized perspective. This transformation is much more comprehensive, for it is a transformation of the perspective itself. It is for this reason that Paul speaks of dying and living, of dying in Adam and being raised in Christ.[19] The achievement orientation, or that of heroism, must die or be transfigured as we saw above. Thus it is an appropriate response to the gospel that one is threatened and "undone" by it. If there were only a rearrangement or an adjustment of ideas (or of data or of beliefs or of actions) involved, one's being or self-understanding remaining unthreatened, response to the gospel would be a relatively simple matter of what Kierkegaard calls a more accurate and deliberate approximation of the ideal.[20] But such is not the case. What is called for by the proclamation of the gospel is a radical shift of the perspective itself, of a change in being which, while involving changes in thought and action, is comprehended in neither of these. Tillich speaks of this change as the presence of New Being, following Paul in II Corin-

---

[19] "For as in Adam all die, so also in Christ shall all be made alive." (I Cor. 15:22.)

[20] For a discussion of Kierkegaard's rejection of the attitude of detachment or reflection as involved in an endless approximation process, see the *Concluding Unscientific Postscript* (Princeton: The Princeton University Press, 1941), esp. Book One, chap. 1.

thians 5:17. One no longer takes himself to be the person who he is according to his criteria or the criteria of his neighbors. These criteria are relative to a cultural-historical situation and are restricted by all the limitedness and conditionedness of that situation. On the contrary, one accepts himself as God accepts and affirms him. Hence a center is given to his being which nothing he does can create for him and from which nothing he thinks or does can separate him. Rudolf Bultmann states the issue quite clearly.

This does not mean that the faithful have a new quality, that they are ethically perfect, or that, their guilt having been canceled, they must now take care for themselves. Rather it simply means that God accepts them as they are. On the other hand, this does not mean that God merely regards the faithful man "as if" he were righteous; on the contrary, by accepting me, God takes me to be a different person than I am; and if I (in faith) let go of what I am in myself, if I affirm God's judgment and understand myself in terms of him, then I really *am* a different person, namely, the one that he takes me to be.[21]

In this case, the question of salvation is put as a question about the integrity of one's being, God's Word received as a word of noumenal power, not of phenomenal objectivity. Faith understood as the entrusting of one's whole self to God's gift of himself dictates a new understanding of the world which both liberates man from having to look to the created world for the ultimate meaning of his existence and also from having to deny the world for the sake of ultimate meaning. As paradoxical as it may seem, faith suspends one from ultimate dependence upon the created world while at

[21] Rudolf Bultmann, "Paul," in *Existence and Faith*, trans. Schubert M. Ogden (New York: Meridian Books, 1960), p. 138.

the same time faith involves one within the world in serious activity. Although salvation comes to man through a worldly form (Jesus is Lord), that which comes to him is from beyond the world.[22] Yet, that which the world in itself does not possess comes to man *through* the world, and the claim of the Christian is that God is present as Christ in the world.

The effect of faith is to free the Christian to affirm the world, to be a man in the world. The Christian man is much more loyal to this orientation, therefore, when all his actions are open toward the meaning of the world as God's creation, in which God is present to heal and redeem, than when he emphasizes "Christian actions" or "Christian thoughts." Consequently, the world may be taken with seriousness as it is, as it really is, as within God's creativity. Man is thus free to study the world and man's status in it, with openness toward the reliable data of sociology, biology, anthropology, history, etc. Faith's affirmation of God's presence in the world does not establish "divine data" in separate fields. The man who trusts God is free from ultimate fear of any of the data about the human situation in the world.

As simple as this point may seem, the difficulty of its acceptance within the religious community is illustrated each year when high school students enter college and subject all the dimensions of their lives to criticism, including the dimension of religion. The person with a religious background has a religious concern, but this concern is conceived in such a way that the particular elements of morality, local social

[22] Perhaps this is a part of Paul's meaning when he writes: "For though we live in the world we are not carrying on a worldly war" (II Cor. 10:3). See also Eph. 6:12.

and political life, and denominational church organization, are accepted as bound up with the religious concern. These persons do not know the biblical point of view but they know many biblical passages which to them seem to support the American Constitution, the free-enterprise system, perhaps the supremacy of one race, or a particular morality about sex and drinking; and they identify this point of view, derived from the culture and substantiated by "proof-texts" from the Bible, as a biblical point of view. For some of them the American way of life is the kingdom of God!

The effect of the college experience, or indeed of any mature experience, is to break up the identity of these elements with one another. Biblical faith is not seen as tied to a particular view on evolution, miracles, anthropology, sociology, economics, and politics. The student is likely to see the inadequacy of the old view more quickly in sociology, biology, and geology, than he sees it in religion. Indeed he usually rejects religion because of the inadequacy of a false biology which he associated with religion. It is the exceptional student who through criticism of religion sees the difference between faith and the world view in which faith expresses itself at a particular time and place. In fact, however, faith is not made problematic by the discovery of any new data in any field of investigation, precisely because faith is not primarily a matter of information within a perspective but a word which we use to designate the reorientation of the perspective or the being of a person toward trust in the Holy.

The illustration of the student suggests the principal characteristic of the Christian in relation to the world. The Christian is free in the world and *for* the world because he is free *from* the world. He is free to think, to feel, and to act completely in terms of the world understood as God's creation, the locus of God's presence, a presence by which he is enabled to understand his life as a gift from One whose power is such that no other one can change or invalidate the gift. He does not live by faith in freedom, a freedom which is always to some extent in the future. He is given freedom within faith, or, rather, freedom is God's gift accepted in faith.

The point has been made elsewhere, but it is important here to suggest explicitly the way faith relates the Christian to the world. The Christian is opened to all the dimensions of the world, to all the dimensions of human existence. He becomes completely relative to the "externals" of life in the sense that he can relate himself to every person in every situation. No inadequacy in a neighbor's ideology, theology, ability, or morality separates a Christian from his neighbor (or the world) because he is called first to *love* the neighbor (the world), not to *reform* him. It is, of course, true that reform, discipline, and morality are important, perhaps of paramount importance on the level of phenomenal history. But on the level of religion all these are important only secondarily. God loves us in spite of *our* wrongness, and the acceptance of his love enables us to be open to affirm the neighbor in spite of *his* wrongness.

The contrast may also be put as between a person who is internally unsure and who seeks to manipulate the externals of the situation (race, nation, success, wealth) to establish himself, on the one hand, and the person who, on the other hand, is internally sure and who, for that reason, is free to deal with the externals of the situation as they are. In the former case a person is so continually having to "prove himself" that people and things invariably get twisted to promote

153

his security. In the latter case, a person is made the beneficiary of the victory in the ultimate warfare; the victory is given to him not for him to guard by the hardest effort but as an inescapable presence it is his joy to affirm. In the ultimate relation, measures of self-defense are unnecessary because neither another person nor oneself can destroy the meaning of one's existence. In preliminary, phenomenal affairs, self-defense has an occasional and proper place, depending upon the particular situation.

It is important to go one step further to show how time is involved in the freedom of the Christian man. The freedom about which we are speaking is not conceptual, but a conceptual consideration is necessary in order to deny a conceptual denial of this freedom. The Christian may speak of freedom as if it were a concept in order to refute a conceptual denial of freedom, but an idea or concept of freedom is never an adequate indication of the Christian understanding of freedom. The freedom of the Christian is not ideational but existential, not a proposition that is eternally true but a gift received within a specific, lived relationship. Freedom is God's desire for all men, but only the man who trusts God knows this. Trust (faith) and freedom are, consequently, events in the flow of time, not ideas above the flow of time. Trust is "lived" and so is freedom.

There is an implication here about man's nature that puts in question the traditional way of understanding man's freedom. We generally speak of God's will, of doing God's will, and of a life of obedience, all of which suggest that God has a specific will for us in every instance which he communicates to man. The suggestion, further, is that God's approval awaits our actual obedience to his will. The focus inevitably turns upon "doing the Christian thing," and there develops a parallel fear of doing wrong. Man's relation to God becomes so specific that God's reality is concentrated in man's capacity to receive and obey moral instructions. The image of the lawgiver and the servant who receives the law and seeks to obey it comes to mind.

The man of faith understands and lives freedom in a transformed perspective in a quite different way. The most important thing for man to do here is not to obey God's specific will or commands, but to accept his own freedom and responsibility to be a man, a center of creativity, an initiator of relationships, a maker of things. Until man takes responsibility for what he does specifically instead of saying that God told him to do it, there is no way for man to "serve" God. God is not interested in man's being any less a man in order to be a Christian. Man is not a man in order to be a Christian, but he is a Christian in order to be a man. That is, his concept of humanness is given him in Christian faith. His freedom to act in full responsibility and dignity is a gift Christ bestows upon him. God is no more interested in giving specific instructions to men than parents are to mature children. His will is not in his "words" but in his "Word." Here the answer is no longer, "you should vote democratic," or "you should marry Jim," or "you should keep Red China out of the United Nations." Rather it is, "consider all the factors in the situation and do what seems to you best to serve the welfare of all the persons involved, remembering my love for you whether the choice is right or not." God's relation to man brings to expression a similar kind of trust. But the specific decision is man's, not God's, a decision taken within love, freedom, trust, and responsibility. The entire process is open to the dimension of the Holy, but the Holy is not localized so as to bear responsibility for man's specific decisions. Every decision is taken within faith and yet man accepts full responsibility for the decision. The presence of God here, then, is real to man's entire being. Because a man is a Christian he is free to do the human thing, the thing most needful for the health and integrity of his neighbor. He is free to "take the world in its stride," to live in the world affirming the world, with no special immunity, no special privilege, and no special professional vocation, for the whole earth is the Lord's. Because a man is a Christian he takes responsibility for his use of freedom in the world. Accepting the gift of a new life, a new being, a life of forgiveness and freedom, he may for the first time take full responsibility for his actions. He, with Luther, is at the same time sinner and forgiven. He is free for responsibility.

IMPLICATIONS FOR THE LIFE
OF THE CHURCH

The cultural role of the church in many situations militates against an appreciation of her peculiar role as church. What might be called "evangelical Protestantism" sees the church as a community of those who now possess the promise of future salvation. Church activity tends to nurture this hope through repentance and belief and good deeds while the saving gospel is proclaimed to the lost. On the other hand "ordinary Protestantism" accommodates the transcendent to the level of a resource for successful and happy living in the present world. It might appear on the surface that the position taken in this book is equivalent to that of "ordinary Protestantism." That is not the intention. The life of the church, like the life of the individual Christian, is a life in positive relation to the world, but a positive relation established by God's action in Christ. No accommodation of the Holy to the world, or of the world to the Holy is intended. But the Holy is affirmed in and through the world.

Again the principal meaning of the transformation of perspective appears to be a change in direction, so that the church is now understood as a community which exists to celebrate or to continue the incarnation by enfleshing God's activity to reconcile the world to himself rather than as a community which assists people to get out of the world to God. God's coming to man is emphasized rather than man's going to God.

Here, too, however, the most important effect of the change is the reconception of the life of the church herself. The mission of the church is to serve mankind, to identify herself with what God is doing in the world, and to do this as a "community of reconciliation," a "body" which becomes, in George W. Webber's words, *God's Colony in Man's World.*[23] Within this understanding, the church is much less concerned with herself, her progress, administrative organization, building, budget, and the like, and much more concerned with the exposure of the whole worldly situation to the light and power of the transcendent. Bonhoeffer saw in the church in Germany a stodginess which manifested itself in several ways: the extremely speculative language of the theologians and preachers; an inordinate selectivity exercised by the church as an "institution for salvation"; a special attention to the upper classes; a detachment from the area of man's primary and

[23]Cf. also *The Church of the Servant,* by Anthony T. Hanson (London: SCM Press, 1962).

actual concerns; a good personal conscience which was far too insensitive; and an embarrassing gullibility in accommodation to the Nazi ideology. "The Church," Bonhoeffer writes, "must get out of her stagnation. We must move out again into the open air of intellectual discussion with the world, and risk shocking people if we are to cut any ice." [24]

In a brief outline of a book which he hoped to survive prison to write, Bonhoeffer speaks caustically about changes in the life of the church which must come about.

The Church is her true self only when she exists for humanity. As a fresh start she should give away all her endowments to the poor and needy. The clergy should live solely on the free-will offerings of their congregations, or possibly engage in some secular calling. She must take her part in the social life of the world, not lording it over men, but helping and serving them. She must tell men, whatever their calling, what it means to live in Christ, to exist for others. And in particular, our own Church will have to take a strong line with the blasphemies of *hybris,* power-worship, envy and humbug, for these are the roots of evil. She will have to speak of moderation, purity, confidence, loyalty, steadfastness, patience, discipline, humility, content and modesty. She must not underestimate the importance of human example, which has its origin in the humanity of Jesus, and which is so important in the teaching of St. Paul. It is not abstract argument, but concrete example which gives her word emphasis and power.[25]

[24] Letter of August 3, 1944.
[25] "Outline for a Book," in *Letters and Papers from Prison,* Macmillan Paperbacks Edition, pp. 239-40. The question of churches receiving support through a system of "religious tax" (*Kirchensteuer*) will seem strange to Americans. There was talk about changing the system in Germany after World War II. But the change was not made and the church-tax system is still in operation. It should be pointed out, however, that neither system is a guarantee against abuse, and both systems have strength. The strength of the free-will offering of the people is that people directly support the church and carry out her work. The danger is a sort of "culture Chris-

Bonhoeffer's statement assumes that there is a difference between the churches as they are and the true church. Making the same assumption, we go further and state a claim as to the proper nature and function of the church. It is not our purpose to document a criticism of the churches as they are. Appalling contrasts with the Protestant churches in America today will be clear enough to the sensitive reader.

Yet there is one basic point underlying many other criticisms one might utter, a point which must be clarified. The American churches, in general, have kept close to the people and the world in which the people live. To that extent American Protestantism apparently illustrates Bonhoeffer's point about how things ought to be. But the sensitive and thoughtful Christian cannot see the Protestant churches in America today as approaching Bonhoeffer's vision of what the church ought to be. Being close to the people, being in the world, and existing for humanity are all vacuous activities unless there is a substance and power of transcendence involved. For the church to continue to use religious terminology without awareness of the transcendent, without compassion for mankind and an insight into what man is, is to engage in deceptive magic. Bonhoeffer's use of "speaking" and "example" are indicative, for together they suggest the embodi-

---

tianity" in which the "voice of the pew dictates the voice of the pulpit," and the transcendent dimension of the Word of God is lost within the voices of men. The strength of the church-tax system is that the church has the money to do her work, and that people with theological competence determine what this proper work is. In post-war Germany the advantage of this system is quite apparent in the ability of the church not only to build (and rebuild demolished) churches, but to do this with studious care to the religious meaning of church architecture. The danger in this system was demonstrated in the Nazi period when the government sought the ultimate loyalty of every pastor whose salary was handled in any way with tax monies.

ment of awareness and acknowledgment of the transcendent (the Beyond in our midst) and a vision of and compassion for the human (existence for humanity).

Perhaps it is unnecessary to say that there is no place for that form of paternalistic self-righteousness on the part of the church which offers the world a pattern and power of success, if the world will accept the church's terms; or which, when there is war, depression, or tragedy, says to the world, "I told you so." The church does not possess a blueprint for the amelioration of the world's ills. But the church does embody God's love of the world and of all people in it, incarnating the meaning of love to a community whose many problems are not thereby all solved, and she continues to live joyfully in celebration of God's Christly action within the world. Consequently, the church in all her particular actions both conceals and reveals, exposes and protects, the mystery of her life. To the world in general, the mystery is exposed and concealed. That is, the church exists to serve humanity and the world, inevitably exposing and expressing the mystery of God's love. At the same time the church does not claim her service or action as Christian, does not require the world to accept God as a condition of receiving the church's action of love. Hence the propositional or confessional dimension of the mystery is concealed even in the act of exposing the mystery.

Within the church herself, on the other hand, the mystery of her existence is revealed and protected. The church does not live on general truth, but on a particular truth which is applicable to all conditions of men. Because there is a particular truth, a particular manifestation of God, a particular act of God, a particular Lord involved in the creation of the church, the church celebrates a particular "revelation" and exercises disciplinary care that those who accept life in this community understand and continue to grow in free loyalty to this particularity. The church is properly reluctant to enact an administrative discipline of her members, but she nevertheless witnesses to a particular base which involves a discipline. No one is forced to become a member of the church, and no one is sent to hell if he is not a member, but accepting membership involves a drastic reorientation of existence to existence-in-Christ, or existence-in-faith. The usual questions one answers in joining a serious organization suggest, although in a superficial way, the important role played by the "discipline" or "protection" of the mystery: "Will you accept what we offer? Will you give what we ask?" In more theological terms Paul urges one not to drink the cup of the Communion to his own judgment;[26] that is, do not drink calculatingly, pretentiously, or insincerely. You are not forced to drink. If you drink, you drink in freedom, and you drink because you may, not because you must. Do not exercise your freedom as a man in such a way that you deliberately avoid affirming what you apparently intend to affirm. This discipline is manifest in various ways in the church, but most crucially in the answer one is asked to give to the invitation to the celebration of the Lord's Supper:

Ye who do truly and earnestly repent of your sins, and are in love and charity with your neighbors, and intend to lead a new life, following the commandments of God, and walking from henceforth in his holy ways; draw near with faith, and take this

---

[26] "Whoever, therefore, eats the bread or drinks the cup of the Lord in an unworthy manner will be guilty of profaning the body and blood of the Lord. For any one who eats and drinks without discerning the body eats and drinks judgment upon himself." (I Cor. 11:27, 29.)

161

holy Sacrament to your comfort: and make your humble confession to Almighty God, devoutly kneeling. (Book of Common Prayer.)

The choice to participate in the Communion is a choice to participate in Jesus Christ and love, and so to participate is to choose against that which denies Christ and love, whatever is anti-Christ, whatsoever is of the nature of brutality or hate. "You cannot drink the cup of the Lord and the cup of demons. You cannot partake of the table of the Lord and the table of demons." (I Cor. 10:21.) Within the true church as a confessing community, the mystery is protected.

The discipline of protection is made necessary by the presence of the mystery. Here one is not dealing with the ordinary, the "canny," the conventional, but with the "unusual," the "uncanny," and the unconventional. The phenomenal form which the revelation assumes is ordinary enough, but that which is manifest in and through the phenomena is of a radically "other" quality from that of ordinary experience. When confronted by the Presence of ultimate concern and significance, one before whom man lives or dies, before whom existence is blessed or damned, man is moved to use the solemn language "Sanctus, Sanctus, Sanctus." Each occasion of worship is a celebration of God's presence in the world in the past, the re-enactment or invocation of his presence now, and the renewal of hope for his presence in the future. As the presence of Christ creates the life of the church, the church acknowledges and protects this presence as *the* treasure of her life, *the* determinative reality of her being.

The church enters the narrow gate (door) Jesus Christ.[27]

[27] Cf. the Gospel of John, chap. 10.

162

But the gate leads to wideness and abundance of life in the world. To insist upon a wide gate or a narrow life is to misunderstand the paradoxical relation of God to the world, the paradoxical nature of the life of the Christian and of the church. It is precisely because of the presence of God in the particular opening of the narrow door (Christ) that one is freed from the world, freed to go "in and out and find pasture." The church acknowledges a particular act of God (Jesus Christ event) as being the manifestation of the meaning of God's relation to all men in all the world, while at the same time insisting upon the freedom of every man to accept or reject this meaning. In all her manifold activities, therefore —proclamation, creation of community, teaching, thanksgiving, hoping, and serving—the church conceals and reveals, exposes and protects, the mystery. She embodies in a community of persons God's activity for the creation, preservation, renewal, and fulfillment of human life and of the world.[28]

AND IF THIS BE TRUE . . .

Assuming that the transformation of perspective actually occurs, what difference does this make? One might readily say, "no difference at all." But one might also say, "all the difference in the world." In a way, both these statements are true. The change makes no difference at all in the data of life, for no Christian biology replaces a non-Christian one. One's gene structure, social problems, intellectual gifts, etc., remain the same. Yet in another sense everything is different because the same data are within the context of a different

[28] For a particularly striking claim of God's act in a political sense of bringing this best human realization of each circumstance, see Paul L. Lehmann, *Ethics in a Christian Context* (New York: Harper & Row, 1963).

understanding and, as a consequence, actually have a different meaning. This view is immediately attractive, for on the basis of it one might set up a series of polar terms suggesting a dialectic or an alternation between those on the one side and those on the other.

Should one do this, however, he would be asserting the equal status of both terms and, by implication, saying that there is neither a personal nor a conceptual resolution of the resulting tension. Such a view would obscure a sharp difference in importance between the two terms. Actually there is no alternation between the data of religion and the data of science, but a radical choice between the historical-personal and the scientific-objective as a primary orientation to life. One puts first trust in either God *or* in the data. There can be only one ultimate trust, one ultimate kind of relationship. Thus the question of how a Christian lives in the world is not resolved by a radical choice between God and the world, or by an alternation between God and the world, but by an affirmation of God's incarnation in the world, God's "presence" in the world to confront man in history with the grace of the transcendent, as a center of meaning and joy for man's life. Such data as are confusing, patternless, and painful are seen as they really are, with no external resolution or amelioration imposed upon them. But a light is manifest within the context of the confusion of the data, giving meaning to human existence in spite of the patternless and the painful. Man is not torn between "data" and "persons"; he is torn between faith and unfaith. The Christian man is called to a way of accepting both his personal existence (and the community of persons) and the realm of things into a wholeness of life. For contemporary man, Paul's contention that in Christ all things

"cohere" has its peculiar thrust at this point.[29] In the final
chapter we will see that this wholeness cannot be a matter of
verification in just any way, and consider in some detail the
particular form or "style" of the life of the Christian in the
world today.

It is the contention of this chapter that the Christian is
passionately involved in and concerned about this world and
all the people in it, that he appreciates and cherishes the vitalities, truths, and beauties of life here and now. He rejects
the interpretation of religion that closes off areas of the world
or dimensions of personal being from the concern of God.
Yet he affirms the world not as it is in itself, whatever that
may be, but as the locus of the creating, sustaining, and healing
presence of God's act in Christ. He is not torn between this
world and the next. He affirms the next world in and through
this one. He is not torn between God above and God below.
He affirms God as a Beyond in our midst. In the truest meaning of the words, the Christian is a "man for others" [30] in,
with, through, and for the world.

Gerhard Ebeling completes a series of lectures to the university community at Zürich with the following:

In conclusion, faith makes the world what it truly is, the creation
of God. It rids the world of demons and myths, and lets it again
be what God wills it to be. Because faith frees us from the world,
it frees us for the world. Because it does not live on the world,
it makes it possible for us to live for the world. Because it puts an

[29] "He is before all things, and in him all things hold together." (Col.
1:17.) See the full passage 1:15-23.
[30] Cf. Robinson, *Honest to God*, chap. 4 (Philadelphia: The Westminster Press, 1963). Cf. also Ronald Gregor Smith, *Secular Christianity*
(New York: Harper & Row, 1966), and Larry Shiner, *The Secularization
of History* (Nashville: Abingdon Press, 1966).

end to the misuse of the world, it opens the way to the right use of the world. Because it breaks the domination of the world, it gives domination over it and responsibility for it. And because it drives out the liking and the misliking of the world, it creates room for pure joy in the world.[31]

But God's presence in and for the world and the meaning of the Christian's presence in and for the world are not to be confused with a systematic order of truth with Christ as the unifying term, or with a moral code in which imitation of Christ is the highest term, or with a promise of happiness and success in the world today with God as a fourth dimension of power. The cross reminds us that the form of God's presence in the world is that of suffering for and with the world. His presence is in complete respect of our freedom, the freedom of a man to deny him and the freedom of a clergyman to be so confused as to serve as "chaplain" to the Ku Klux Klan, the freedom of a man to attempt to destroy others as well as himself. Christ is the one in whom "all things hold together" in that the love of God for the world is present in him. Suffering and joy characterize the life of Christ and the life of the Christian. The treasure is in earthen vessels, "love suffers long," for this world is not the kingdom of God, but the kingdom of God has come to this world.

In sum, then, there are three ideas for which a revision in the Christian's attitude toward the world is crucial—sacredness, creativity, faith. The Christian come of age living in a world come of age affirms the sacred not as a place or time over against other places or times, but as the concrete appearance of the sacred which gives a center to all places and

[31] *The Nature of Faith*, p. 161.

times.[32] He affirms human creativity not only within what the canons of a particular standard of propriety or morality designate "good," but across the entire spectrum of possibilities which existence in God's grace allows. He understands faith not as separating him from the world or from evil but as acceptance of God's presence within the complex of good and evil to sustain, deepen, dignify, enrich, and humanize life.

[32] See Mircea Eliade, *The Sacred and the Profane* (New York: Harper & Row, 1959).

VI
The Success and Failure of Love

> I will not cease from mental fight,
>   Nor shall my sword sleep in my hand,
> Till we have built Jerusalem
>   In England's green and pleasant land.
>   (William Blake, *Milton*.)

To the end of history the peace of the world, as Augustine observed, must be gained by strife. It will therefore not be a perfect peace.[1]

THE PROBLEM

Faith involves a freedom from the world as a structure in which we seek security; but faith means taking the world seriously as the place where our actual life is to be lived. In-

---

[1] Reinhold Niebuhr, *Moral Man and Immoral Society* (New York: Charles Scribner's Sons, 1932), p. 256.

sofar as he acts in faith, the Christian acts in obedience to God and self-forgetting love. Yet these are not the powers that move the world as we see it. Or rather, if we simply observe the world, we can see in it some aspects of mutuality and self-giving, but we cannot see that these are in any way ultimate. Yet the concern of faith and love for the "other," the concrete person existing here in the world, drives action that arises out of faith to try to enter into the world, into the tangible network of forces that make up and environ the life of the "other." Here lies the paradox of the application: Christian action tries to do something that in one sense cannot be done. Action arising out of faith aims to transform existence toward the vision of faith and love, and it claims to be real action. Yet the world, the actual social environment, though it may respond temporarily to an act of love, is directed primarily by other forces, and the total transformation of existence into the "pure present" of love never endures. If this is the situation, what results can be hoped for from action in faith, and what ways can be found for intelligently relating the intention of self-giving love to the largely unloving reality of the world in which we live? An earlier generation could ease this tension by means of the belief in progress. The gradual transformation of life, the earthly coming of the kingdom of God through the channel of the devoted efforts of believers, or perhaps of men of good will generally, would close the gap between existence as it must come to be in God's purpose, and existence as it is. Few people believe this today, although the power of the belief in progress still manifests itself in a special form in Marxism. Today, however, Christians realize that they must take more seriously the gap between what life is and what, in faith, they know it is intended to be. Their action cannot permanently transform historical existence; at best it may temporarily renew some aspect of it.

To explore the paradox of application, we shall set forth briefly the story of an American Christian who lived out, to a remarkable degree, one pattern of Christian action which is still powerful and suggestive. This concrete example will help us understand both the possibilities of Christian action and the framework within which it takes place.

AN INSTANCE: JOHN WOOLMAN

For an example of love in action, let us look at the American Quaker John Woolman.[2] Little known today, and never widely known, this man who lived before the Revolutionary War can nevertheless serve exceptionally well to bring into focus the claim of Christian action. The fact that he lived in a different age means that he may appear merely as a quaint, old-fashioned figure, and of course it means as well that we cannot use him directly to illuminate the problems of our own time. But what he did, and the way in which he did it, can serve as a thoroughly serious and relevant instance of the issues involved in getting from the intention of being "there" for the "other" over into the concrete historical existence in which the "other" lives. The distance at which we stand from him will also help us to see some things about Christian action that are not so easy to see in our own situation. On the surface Woolman may seem unmodern because of his self-conscious faith, and because he belonged to a somewhat "separated"

---

[2] John Woolman, 1720-72, was a New Jersey Quaker whose action and writing focused on the realization of the human meaning of slavery and on awakening his fellow Quakers to the impossibility of reconciling Christian faith with anything that had such human meaning.

group, as the Society of Friends was in the eighteenth century. But more profoundly, Woolman's creative struggle to find his way into an unsettled question of his day still remains a most suggestive one for persons living in a situation of relative freedom. His pattern of action can thus also make us more aware of the question of the setting within which men act, which—as we see today—often may not allow the freedom which our common American idea of Christian action assumes.

Woolman's life is all the more serviceable as an example because the situation into which he directed his energies has increasingly become a crucial one in the nearly two centuries that have passed since his death: the problem of the relation between white and Negro. Woolman came upon this situation, of course, not as the race problem but as the problem of slavery. What makes him particularly important for our thinking is that the wrongness of this situation did not dawn upon Woolman out of a concern for the large-scale processes and structures of society, but in the course of his probing the meaning of his own choices. He did not begin with the question of social utility but with personal responsibility.

In Woolman's time, the problem of the relation between white and Negro was just beginning to be an obvious problem. The conscience of the day accepted the inequalities of slavery with little conscious uneasiness. Even within his own religious group, the Society of Friends, or Quakers, slavery was largely taken for granted, though Woolman was far from the first to protest against it. A major thrust of the Friends' testimony had been toward the equality of all before God, and this testimony had already found important expression in other aspects of the social pattern. For instance, the Quakers were practically unique at the time in recognizing an equality of men and women in the management of the affairs of the Society. Woolman was only one of those who were coming to see the injustice of slavery. Thus we must remember that Woolman did not act as an isolated individual. His insights were won by taking seriously and working through the heritage which his particular Christian tradition brought to him, and his action is important for us, not because he was the only one who was concerned, but because he has left in his *Journal* a transparent record of the interplay between his inner life and its outward expression in acts of love.

A farmer's son and the proprietor of a shop, Woolman encountered the problem which opened his eyes to the claims and difficulties of Christian obedience and love without consciously searching for it. As one of the better-educated men in the community, he was asked by neighbors and friends to draw up their wills and other legal documents. At times these documents included provisions for the inheritance or sale of slaves, and after considerable struggle of conscience Woolman found that he had to decline to write such documents. If it was wrong for the system to allow one person to have so much power over another, then he would have to stay clear of any involvement in the system of slavery, so far as he could.[3] As his life developed, Woolman carried his purpose of "staying apart" from involvement in slavery to

[3] He expressed himself in this way: "Deep rooted customs, though wrong, are not easily altered; but it is the duty of all to be firm in that which they certainly know is right for them. . . . Man, as man, knows not what shall be after him, nor has he any assurance that his children will attain to that perfection in wisdom and goodness necessary in every absolute governor; hence it is clear to me that I ought not to be the scribe where wills are drawn in which some children are made absolute masters over others during life." (John Woolman, *Journal*, ed. Janet Whitney [Chicago: Henry Regnery Company, 1950], p. 33.)

extreme limits. He gave up the use of sugar because it was produced by slave labor, and when he stayed at a plantation where slaves did the work, he would leave some money rather than simply accept his host's hospitality. His non-participation in society was extended to many other things. Because he had scruples about dyed cloth (since the dyes were mainly produced by slave labor, and impressed him as unnecessary luxury), Woolman refused to wear clothes made of normal colors, and set himself apart by wearing only plain, undyed clothes. And he was not a person with much of a sense of humor, so that some of the cases of his clearing himself from association with evil are now somewhat comical to us. For instance, we see him in a tavern where a crowd has assembled to see a juggler, reasoning calmly with the audience which had come to be entertained that it was wrong to give money to men whose life, as he said, was of no use—and, of course, convincing no one.

But the struggle to disengage himself, expressed in a form which can be negative and withdrawing, in Woolman's case was fully in balance with a movement toward involvement, toward giving himself into the situation to which he could not consent. His involvement expressed itself primarily in a series of journeys across the colonies (and finally to England where he died) to testify against the practice of slavery.

As noted in the previous chapter, the history of Christian withdrawal from life has been so deeply marked by self-protectiveness that we may easily overlook this function of concern which it often has. For Woolman, his disengagement was not merely protective; it was a way of saying, a form of speech: Look what we are doing when we do these things which I feel called upon to renounce. Our criticism of Chris-

173

tian retreat from the world must not lead us to undervalue the possibilities of this intention of disengagement.

Each new period requires a new vision of our failures, and the attempt to stay apart from the failures of society is a recurrent form of declaring what those failures are.

A reader of his record of his visits in the *Journal* cannot help being deeply impressed by John Woolman's way of excluding his own personal status from consideration. There are those who build themselves a status in the project they serve. Woolman's effort of self-understanding and self-discipline was turned in the other direction, to try to be sure that nothing of his own preference stood in the way of the honest and humble performance of the task in hand. On the one hand, as he tells the story in his *Journal* he scarcely indicates the role which he himself played in the changing position of the Society of Friends about slavery. On the other hand, in the actual situation he did not shrink from speaking very frankly in opposition to the practice of slavery by his hosts and associates, yet he did it in a way that was singularly free from resentment or defensiveness. He did not use his concern as an opportunity to build his own reputation. His concern that those who were pressing for a good cause should not do so as a projection of their own status is both charmingly and powerfully stated in his old-fashioned language many times in his *Journal,* as for instance, when he remarks that if those who "at times were under sufferings on account of some scruples of conscience [who were discriminated against or looked down on because of their conscientious protest] kept low and humble, and in their conduct in life manifested a spirit of true charity, it would be more likely to reach the witness in others, and be of more service in the church, than if their sufferings were attended with a contrary spirit and conduct." [4] In Woolman's case, this exclusion of his self and success from consideration was not something easily won. He struggled with himself repeatedly on this point, and we find him rebuking himself for, as he says on one occasion, "saying more than was required of me" (i.e., injecting his own righteous resentment into his message), and striving for weeks afterward to re-establish his base in a goodness that was given to him in faith and not in his own assertiveness.

If we asked what role his Christian faith played in enabling a largely self-educated man, somewhat cut off from the currents of public life, to come to see something which today is obvious to every honest conscience, we can answer this question from what Woolman says in his *Journal* along two related lines: (1) he found in faith a liberation from convention or custom, which seemed to him to be a mask behind which men easily evaded the responsibility of fully confronting the human situation they were in,[5] and (2) he found that he was free from himself, to identify himself with another person and to see what it was like to be in the other person's position.[6]

In acting for his concern as he did, Woolman represented the best of his own religious tradition, for from the beginning the Quakers had the faith that a new and fuller community of men was possible, and that men of faith could open the eyes

[4] *Ibid.,* p. 84.

[5] Cf. his remarks about the need for standing against "deep-rooted customs," cited in note 2; it is in this framework of social responsibility that he applies the Puritan-Quaker language about "the danger of conforming to the fashions of the world." (*Journal,* p. 142, quoting another Friend.)

[6] "Desires were renewed in me . . . to embrace every opportunity of being inwardly acquainted with the difficulties of my fellow-creatures." (*Ibid.,* p. 177.)

175

of others to this possibility by persuasion. At the same time, the insight that steps must be taken to prevent future generations from abusing power as the present generation is abusing it implies a clear recognition of the necessity for a firm and enforced social pattern to channel and limit the use of power, the necessity of using power to meet power. The history of the American struggle with the question of the relation between white and Negro shows how seldom the problem has been confronted in Woolman's terms, that is, within a simple but radical identification with the human existence of the disadvantaged group, and an effort to persuade others to change their way of living in accord with their insight into their real personal responsibilities. The overall story raises important questions about the possibility of action being as "pure" as Woolman wished it to be. The attempt to influence the structure of society in order to limit the abuses of power carries action beyond the sphere of pure persuasion.[7] To this question of compromise we shall return. At the same time, Woolman's deeply religious insight was able to uncover a new meaning for justice in his society, and in this he points to a central function of Christian action, to initiate concern in a neglected area. That the new way of thinking about justice can then often be retained and also expanded, on the basis of mutual self-interest and without direct relation to Christian action as such, indicates the temporary nature of Christian action, and is also a reminder that its intention is not simply

---

[7] Woolman seldom attempted to exert political power, in keeping with a trend within the Society of Friends of his day to withdraw from politics precisely because the political sphere involved them in the compromise of their principles. But we do find him urging the New England Yearly Meeting to put pressure on the Rhode Island legislature to put an end to the importation of slaves (*Journal,* pp. 99-101).

to improve the physical-social circumstances in which men live, but to act in a way which will disclose to men the real claim and promise of God for them.

One of the reasons why Woolman is an attractive example of Christian action is that, within his chosen restricted sphere, he did achieve results. He and others of like conviction led the Society of Friends to a decision that ownership of slaves was contrary to their understanding of faith, and this result was achieved during his own lifetime. For the most part the change took place by persuasion, though a few who could not agree were excluded from membership in the Society. But in choosing Woolman as a model of Christian action, it is not intended to suggest that this favorable outcome is built into the way in which such action is related to the society in which it acts. A modern example like the German Protestant Dietrich Bonhoeffer would show us the same interaction of faith and love, the same grasp of action as for the "other," and yet in a setting where the actual short-term result was failure. Christian action is deeply involved with hope, a point to which we shall return below. But this hope is not a conviction that "my" personal project of action shall succeed.

THE RENEWAL OF JUSTICE BY LOVE

Thus Woolman's sensitivity to the situation of the "other" enabled him to reach a new judgment about justice. This is a recurring function of Christian action—to be the vehicle through which love criticizes the accepted standard of justice, and opens the eyes of a society to the possibility of a new understanding of justice. The concern for the "other," as he is seen in the moment, moves toward a concern for the continuing structures within which the "other," and others like

177

him, must live. As Woolman put it, "those who have faithfully attended to the nature and spirit of the reformation . . . have not only to instruct others by their example, . . . but also to use means to prevent their successors from having so much power to oppress others." [8] It is this aim of "using means to prevent [men] from having so much power to oppress others" that repeatedly brings action out of the purely personal sphere into the attempt to shape the continuing structures of power.

Woolman is a model of this way of understanding the achievement of Christian action, which has been in American Christianity the principal way of thinking about it: Christian action as the uncovering of a new standard of justice, which, once presented, could commend itself to the society and become, perhaps through a long period of struggle, the accepted pattern of behavior. This way of understanding the creative contribution of action out of faith need not, of course, be limited to Christianity; one thinks of the work of Gandhi and Vinoba Bhave in India. But it has been a particularly significant way of thinking in the broad stream of Puritan Christianity which has done so much to shape the American way of thinking. It presupposes (1) that the openness and inner freedom of concern for the "other" reach out also into the social structures, (2) that there is a structure of justice which can be reshaped, and (3) that there is a degree of outer freedom to speak, act, and bring pressure to bear on the pattern of society.

About the first point, all that need be said here is that while Christians have not always perceived the openness toward the other in relation to the structures of society, an important

[8] John Woolman, *Journal*, p. 150.

side of Christian tradition has had a strong sense that the person is not to be understood or loved simply as an isolated individual, but that his life is made up in good measure of the patterns within which he lives, so that these patterns of social life are a valid and important field of expression of action in Christian love. The tradition is somewhat overshadowed today, partly because of the narrow legalism of some of its "puritanical" expressions, partly because of the unjustified optimism of some Christian social reformers, partly because of the vigorous upsurge of theology stemming from the Lutheran tradition with its more static conception of the relation between the person and the social structure within which he lives, and partly because we are now so keenly aware that there are unforeseen by-products of any conscious effort to reshape society. The criticisms of religious reformers made from these points of view have a good deal of strength, as do the similar criticisms of the humanistic and secular reform movements which are themselves in part the offspring of the view of Christian action which we see in Woolman. But the value of this model of Christian action is by no means cancelled out by these criticisms. A fresh and sober grasp of Christian action as the renewal of justice through love is one of the principal lines through which Christian faith may speak to the life of our time. For the explosive social changes of our times, if nothing else, compel us to interpret our concern for the other person in terms of the structures within which he lives.

At the same time it is important to remember that not all Christians are in the same situation, and social change and social freedom do not always go together. Love as action that challenges and intends to renew the understanding of justice in a society cannot function to bring about social change without a degree of freedom. This is not to say that Christian faith needs a favorable environment. But it is a reminder that Christians living where democratic freedom allows them opportunity to speak and act in pressure upon established standards of justice need to exercise far more understanding than they have often shown toward Christians whose freedom of action is more severely limited. There are situations in which it is irresponsible to direct one's energies into pressure on the government and society. American Christians as a whole have given little thought to what responsible Christian action is in situations of non-freedom. A Czech Christian remarked bitterly to an American, "According to you, we ought not to exist." That is, the naïve American Christian believes that there is a certain acceptable form of society within which a Christian can live, and he is suspicious of those who live in different situations. Eastern European Christians share with Christians in parts of Asia—and, possibly before long, Africa —a struggle to exist within forms of society that intend to choke them off.[9] But this situation only makes all the clearer the fact that men's lives are in large measure constituted by the structures within which they exist. And it reminds us as well that freedom to act is always a mysterious quantity. There is no sure way to know whether there is any result to be achieved. Nor is it possible to act by an absolute standard of right. The Christian is called to act to the margin of his freedom, never knowing just where that margin is. We see here a connection with the question of suffering discussed in the final chapter.

Christian action thus expresses the freedom of faith from

[9] Cf. *Here for a Reason: Christian Voices in a Communist State,* ed. Elisabeth Adler (New York: The Macmillan Company, 1964).

the existing pattern, which enables the man of faith to be a
critic, while at the same time it expresses his serious concern
for the pattern, as the structure within which the "other"
finds his life. Such an understanding of how love moves over
to a concern for justice must be a major way of thinking
about Christian action. A figure like Woolman can help us
understand its possibilities for our own situation. Nonetheless,
it would be one-sided to leave the impression that the predomi-
nant expression of Christian love is its movement to challenge
existing standards of justice through the insight of love. For
this point where acts of love become visible, so to speak, in
the critical areas of a society's life, is the fruit of a continuous,
inconspicuous openness of love in unreflective response to men
as they are in their various situations. On a purely quantitative
basis (if we may venture to speak in such a way) the number
of acts of Christian love that are intended to reconstitute the
pattern of men's relations to one another is a small fraction
of the whole. For this kind of action, the concrete social circumstances are taken seriously because the person is taken
seriously. The aim is not simply to make things comfortable
for the other, but so to act that, if possible, the action may be
a sign telling him something about himself and about the
mystery in which his life is rooted. This does not mean that
one has to be a model parent in order to be justified in acting
for better facilities for the education of children. But it does
mean that unless actions in the public realm are sustained by
and grounded in a field of concrete, humble, inconspicuous
openness to men and women, they cannot adequately express
Christian action. It is a severe shortcoming of the "reform-
ing and improving" model of "Christian" that it is so often
understood in isolation from this underlying, continuing, and

basic function of affirming the other in his given situation, an affirmation that is intended to help make possible his relation to true, transcendent reality. For most of us, action of this less conspicuous sort will be the main way in which we give expression to faith. The prophetic critic who stands out in sharp challenge to the society as a whole represents the less articulate rest of us, opens our eyes to what we should have been able to see all along, and confronts us with the challenge of deciding on action that may bring to more adequate expression the claim of love in the area he can see. But he likewise is dependent upon the less articulate group, and unless his intention of love stands in continuity with theirs, he can easily become a bigoted, self-expressive "messiah."

THE NEED FOR COMPROMISE

Another aspect of Christian action also becomes apparent in the instance of Woolman, seen in connection with the later developments in the American struggle with this problem. That is, that the "model" situation of someone like Woolman, who was a quickener of a social standard of justice through insight and personal concern, is in some ways more easily lived out before the issue becomes a public one. In Woolman's time, the issue which concerned him was not a great public issue with lines already drawn. He could make his own way to what he found to be the heart of the issue. The continuing history of Negro-white relations has shown how immensely complicated and compromised such issues become. Part of the story may be viewed under the heading already suggested: the renewal of justice by love. But it has been a sad self-deception on the part of white Americans when they have thought that the problem in its overall history could be understood from this point of view. For large-scale changes to come about, other forces than the personal devotion of Christian love must come into play, and, furthermore, justice is not achieved simply by the generosity of the advantaged group, but by creating a situation in which all groups can press their competitive claims. Most situations in which Christian action enters into the public realm thus involve a large degree of compromise with these other forces.

The free, uncompromising pioneer of Christian action can reveal the intention of Christian action more clearly than can the more limited efforts of those who enter into a situation already the scene of power conflicts and endeavor to make some effort within the power struggle. But most public action is of the latter sort, and must be if the insights already won are to be worked through. The "Christianness" of an action cannot be judged by its disengagement from compromise. All such disengagement is relative; even Woolman could not completely disengage himself from involvement in the system of slavery. Besides, the situation may not permit disengagement. This is so in a double sense, with reference to the past and with reference to the possibilities of the future.

The situation, viewed toward the past, may not permit disengagement, because one's prior responsibilities may allow only a limited amount of energy to be directed to the situation in question. The stock illustration would be, of course, that a person's family responsibilities may prevent him from embarking on a venturesome disengagement from the traditional patterns of life in his society. While the responsibilities of the family have no doubt often provided an excuse or escape from confronting the urgent claim of a new responsibility in the present moment, yet one cannot honestly enter this relationship without accepting the limitations which it places on the acceptance of other responsibilities. Most of the claims made on us do not come merely from momentary or emergency events, but demand time and the channeling of energy for their fulfillment. In this sense it is inevitably true that the past limits our freedom to make a completely new response, disengaged from the prior responsibilities and traditions of the past.

There is also a limit on disengagement when the situation is viewed toward the future. Among other factors in a decision, the possible results have to be considered. This is not to say that the choice is decided solely by the chance of success; but since action is undertaken for the "other," the weighing of the probable results for the other is an inescapable factor in the decision. In many cases, the only way in which we can see a possibility that action will do something for the other is by attempting something far less than a complete resolution of the problem, and by making use of forces far different from Christian love, and even remote from an ideal standard of justice.

Thus, action for the other stands constantly before the threat of "evaporation," of being drawn into developments where it will be absorbed and forgotten. Indeed, this constantly happens and must inevitably happen, whether the outcome of the generous action is a success or a failure. The personal meaning of action can only be sustained by successive acts of renewal. One might conclude from this that the framework of action, and even the results of action, are insignificant, that only the intention counts. But we have seen that the self cannot realistically be understood apart from the structures in which it exists, so that action on the structure is an inevitable result of concern for the other, even though the personal meaning of this effort to change structures tends to decay.

THE SUPPORT OF ACTION BY HOPE

If we recognize the temporary character of personal action in concern for the other, and if we see that concern for the other leads not only to direct action on behalf of the immediate needs of a concrete individual, but also to action which aims to alter the situation in which the individual other, and others like him, live, we must come back once more to the perplexing problem: what do we hope for in terms of results? No specific result can be guaranteed if we recognize the freedom of response on the part of the other person; furthermore, if action for the other passes through the indirect channels of political and economic struggle, compromise with men of varying purposes, and the erosion of time in which original purposes may be weakened or transformed, what prospect is there that the original spontaneous and open intention can speak as the results of action develop? How necessary are results if the spirit of real openness is to be maintained?

Woolman's freedom to act, and his concern for others, were rooted in a prophetic faith in the lordship of God. He believed that injustice could not continue indefinitely, that a divine judgment would show itself upon the situation he found if it was allowed to continue: "this trade and way of life . . . appeared to me as a dark gloominess hanging over the land; and though now many do willingly run into it, yet in future the consequences will be grievous to posterity," [10] was his way of expressing this faith. Correspondingly, he held that

[10] John Woolman, *Journal,* p. 20.

there may be a meaningful positive succession in good acts: "The uprightness of the first reformers [i.e., the leaders of the Protestant Reformation] to the light and understanding given them tended to open way for sincere-hearted people to proceed further afterward." [11] In other words, despite the evil and tragedy in the world he found it still God's creation; and God's rule was manifest historically, not in a morally rational interpretation of contemporary events, but in the faith that contemporary events would have an outcome that would manifest God's righteousness. Love and hope are thus intimately interwoven for Woolman, not in the sense that he believed a concrete act of his own would succeed, but in the sense that he believed his own action to reflect, however imperfectly, a goodness given to him which would one day come to be the only reality. Not only so, but he believed that the common historical experience of men partially reflected the divine judgment. He could commit himself to his calling because he could understand his own efforts as carried by and reflecting a God to whom he was committed.

Secularized versions of this hope are widely reflected in the culture of the United States, and the conviction that there will be an outcome for action on behalf of the other largely accounts for the fact that American culture recognizes a place for such action. Indeed, in our common American understanding, such action easily fuses into a commonsense view that doing right is that which will benefit society as a whole. But here, too, the decision for another goal than immediate self-interest is upheld by hope, by the conviction that the forces at work in society are moving toward making a fuller life for all our citizens a possibility.

[11] *Ibid.*, p. 149.

There is a tremendous difference between the fundamentally religious hope of Woolman, in which all human structures are subject to God's judgment, and the vaguer secular hope of much of America, that men of good will can achieve a better situation for themselves and others. But in both views hope is a significant spring of action. The question must be confronted: how well can love endure when the familiar forms of hope are stripped away? Or when there is no hope left? American secular optimism rests on shaky foundations; the Europe of the period between World War I and World War II stands to Americans as a constant reminder of how men may react when their hope for orderly and reasonable progress is shaken.

To this question the answer of faith cannot, of course, be predictive. No one can say in advance how men will respond to despair and hopelessness, or whether a rootage for openness to the other can be uncovered that will be deep enough to maintain it as a power of action in the collapse of traditional securities that apparently lies ahead. But faith can speak about what it means to act in hope or in the search for hope, and such speaking can call men to open themselves to a deeper grounding of their love, when the traditional reciprocal grounding of mutual love (you help me, I help you) is threatened.

The question is urgent for us because the older Christian understanding of God's rule of the world (expressed, for instance, by Woolman), is severely weakened today. Few Christian thinkers can affirm the continuity of social justice in time in such a way that we can look forward to good or bad consequences for our good or bad actions in society, as Woolman could. Or, if the continuity of justice in social history is maintained, this is done with such reserve and caution that justice can scarcely be expected to apply in a given situation or problem. Furthermore, the otherworldly dimension of traditional Christian thought, the hope for a fulfillment in another order of reality, has been so severely criticized as irresponsible and unrealistic that many Christian thinkers have largely eliminated this dimension of the Christian tradition from their thought.

Recognizing the danger of too easy a theoretical comment on the hard business of honest living, we must nonetheless say that the particular crisis of faith in which we find ourselves does not destroy the intimate connection of love and hope. There will, perhaps, be many who can open themselves to the reality of faith only at the point of love, and who will not be able to express an articulate hope. Still, hope and love are inextricably woven together; an act of love is at the same time an affirmation of hope for the person loved.

The decline of hope may indeed open the way to the rebirth of a more deeply grasped hope-in-faith. The loss of hope is largely the result of the loss of faith in the future of *my own existence* and its consequences. So far as we speak of personal existence only from our own isolated point of view, we have no ground for hope, nor is there hope for the assured continuation of one's projects in the progress of the community. Christian faith is no simple promise of life *for us*. It means precisely facing up to the fact that in ourselves we have no continuing existence. But when we are concerned for something else than our own existence, we can come again to hope. When we are "engaged," drawn out of ourselves *for* the other's existence, when we glimpse the possibility of another life, then we face the real tension in our own existence, but we also

see for the other the reality of goodness that we cannot see
for ourselves. In Christian faith, this tension between the
struggle to affirm ourselves and the effort to affirm the
other's existence is not resolved by a simple internal discipline
or success in self-acceptance. To exist "in Christ" is to participate in a power which is fully given to the affirmation of the
other and which accepts and transforms a self in spite of his
failure in both self-affirmation and other-affirmation. "For
the love of Christ controls us, because we are convinced that
one has died for all; therefore all have died. And he died for
all, that those who live might live no longer for themselves
but for him who for their sake died and was raised." (II Cor.
5:14-15.) Real existence is openness, being there to help the
other one make a real life of his life. In this vast and seemingly
meaningless universe, this simple, humble openness is the
ultimate reality, the reality of God himself. This is eternal
life, which, in however fragmentary a way, becomes our life
in Christ.

Thus, Christian hope is not hope for the survival or significant impact of *my existence,* but faith in the triumph of
God's will. About this hope, there is only one thing we can
say: love endures, the love that reaches out and sustains other
lives. Fragile and imperfect as it is in our world, it is the
real. One cannot meet this love simply as a promise of one's
own survival, but there is, in being drawn into the purpose of
God, a meeting with that humble, unobtrusive goodness which
is real, and which will come to be the only reality. And as we
glimpse, through these bits of true openness which are given
to us, the intention and possibilities, and fragmentary actuali-
ties of this love in others, we see that which will not be lost
or abandoned, but which will in God's own way be renewed to

a higher order of life. The Christian faith in the resurrection does not find its point of leverage in the faith in "my own resurrection," but in the faith that the personal existence of the "other" is taken so seriously by God that he will renew it to life.

Thus, the precariousness of our situation, while it may well dismay the hope for self-fulfillment, does not make impossible that deeper hope which is the companion of self-forgetting love. Such a hope in the ultimate affirmation of the goodness that sustains our own goodness is very different from the hope for a changed structure of human relations as the result of action. These two kinds of hope have fallen apart in our world, but they are not irrelevant to each other. It is by engagement with the other that we may be set free from the false, escapist sort of hope. At the same time, by engagement with the other we affirm our ultimate hope for those whose lives enlist our energies. Such a stance can form a ground, a basis, for a clear and open look at the kinds of hope we may have for changes in the structures of life.

We may summarize by distinguishing between three sorts of result for which one may hope as he engages in action : results affecting oneself, results in the changed situation of others, and results in the form of a declaration or witness to what one stands for. As far as results affecting oneself are concerned, they may be of the negative sort already mentioned, a preserving of what one stands for against the eroding effects of the inner and outer forces which challenge it. It will be a continual concern of any action that springs from faith to maintain the distinctiveness of its point of origin. But if this becomes a primary goal, the result will be a rigid and isolated faith, as the history of Christianity abundantly shows. It is the characteristic of action springing from faith that at its most focused point it loses this concern for its own preservation. "He that saves his life shall lose it." Another sort of result affecting oneself is the result of mutual benefit, in which the spontaneous giving of love is met by an answering response of acceptance and the creation of a community. Toward this sort of result, the action of faith will be open but not demanding. It is a natural hope that there should be a response to one's giving, but to expect or demand it destroys the openness of the relationship. "Love your enemies," we read in the Gospels. "Love your enemy, and you will have no enemy," is the commonsense version of this saying in an early Christian writing. Like so many Christians of later times, this rewriting has transformed the radical demand of Jesus into a predictable result, and thereby changed its meaning. Life does not provide a guarantee that this result of mutual reinforcement will come, though it is natural to hope for it, and it may come.

Considering the possibility of results that change the structures in which men's lives are lived brings us to some of the most difficult problems of action arising from faith. Here the paradox of application can be seen at its most perplexing. The powers that dominate the continuing structures of psychological and social life are so different from the short-lived intention of self-giving that it is hard to see how self-giving action can enter into the world of these relationships. But if we understand the present as constituted by possibilities arising from the past, but not completely determined by them, we can see how self-giving action can inject a new direction into a concrete present, particularly when the time is ripe, when circumstances have brought a problem to the surface

191

which calls for decision. Such self-giving cannot itself become a permanent or dependable part of the continuing process, for it must by its nature be renewed in each situation. But there are times when it may open a new direction to the development of the more stable patterns in which men relate themselves to one another (the "renewal of justice by love"). Such a result cannot be assured in advance; it depends on the responses to the action arising from faith. And, of course, in any actual case, the results that emerge are also shaped by the understanding of the more stable structures that inform the action arising from faith. Good intentions are not enough. If the "power structure" within which one works is not realistically understood, the results of action will be deflected accordingly. And it must be said as well that there will be many situations in which the external freedom to bring pressure to bear on these structures will not be present. Thus the vision of faith impels men so to act as to change, not only their personal relations, but the whole structure of existence. Yet the structure cannot be totally altered; it continually slips back to its self-interested level. But it may be renewed, particularly at critical moments, by action in the freedom arising from faith, even though there can be no guarantee of this result.

Finally, the result of declaration or witness must be noticed, particularly because with our pragmatic temper we so easily overlook it. From the point of view of action that springs from the conviction of faith, all our doing is intended also to be a saying. The profound reversal or challenge of the self which it finds in faith does not permit it simply to act for another, in the sense that the other only needs some external thing done for him. The acting is also a saying, which means that it intends to communicate the basis from which it itself arises. "Testifying," "witnessing"—these words have fallen into a certain disrepute because they have been used in a very narrow sense, often not much related to the real claims of life. But they say something inescapable about action arising from faith. Such action intends to say something to and about the person for whom something is done. And this result is often open when outright action upon social relationships is not.[12] In any case, this is the final goal of Christian action whether or not it succeeds in its concrete social goal, and it is equally important where the actual social venture succeeds.

The Double Movement of Freedom: Disengagement and Re-engagement

In our illustration, Christian action was made effective through a very radical separation from conventional patterns. By turning to a figure like Woolman to illustrate how radical openness to the other may become a factor in action, do we mean that the action of self-forgetting love can be manifest only in a radical break with convention and ordinary life? In a very real sense this is so, although most of the time this freedom will express itself in personal and inconspicuous ways. It is precisely because Woolman so well illustrates this aspect of the demand of love that he is so relevant an example for us. For the usual relation of the self to the continuous patterns of life is that these patterns become a protection against too much claim from other lives. Sharp awareness of the other carries with it—if it is to be awareness leading to action—a freedom from this "cocoon" function of the conventional pat-

[12] See the quotations from Johannes Hamel on pp. 94-95.

terns of life. Woolman expressed his freedom in a pattern of "staying away," of isolating himself from evil, a pattern that has been subjected to very harsh criticism because it has so often been an expression of fear and of a retreat from grappling with the issue. Furthermore, separating oneself from what is believed to be wrong can be a very self-centered moral attitude. And the practices which Christians have identified as wrong have often been rather unimportant ones—regulation of the external details of life. In addition, dissociation from what is judged wrong has often been an expression of a shallow moralism which held that "if only other people would do as I do, the problem would be solved." But if we are free enough ourselves from our own fears, we can penetrate beyond this negative meaning of withdrawal and see its deeper intention of speaking, of disclosing the reality of a situation which most people accept too easily. For us the older patterns of withdrawal may not be viable, but the intention is still valid, and we shall have to find new ways of expressing this "word of non-conformity."

We have seen that in Woolman's case the movement of withdrawal from "the world" was fully balanced by a movement of re-engagement. This double movement is built into the action of love, however varied the specific pattern it takes may be. The contemporary reaction against a typical Protestant moralism must not blind us to the powerful meaning of the claim of love to separate us from that which prevents life for others. Freedom from convention is so easily understood negatively—freedom not to be conventional—that this positive and disciplined meaning of freedom from convention may easily elude us. The freedom to be truly open to the other always carries with it a demand to separate oneself from the protective patterns of mere convention, but this is a structured, disciplined freedom, which involves both staying away from the world and re-entering it for the sake of the other.

The stance which we have illustrated from a previous age is shown in our contemporary world by William Stringfellow, who tells of his experience as a lawyer in Harlem.

To practice law in Harlem requires more than a professional identification with these kinds of cases. It involves more than knowledgeability about the neighborhood, and something different from just sympathy for the people of the ghetto. Humanitarian idealism is pretentious in Harlem, and turns out to be irrelevant. It is, rather, more important to experience the vulnerability of daily life. It is necessary to enter into and live within the ambiguity, and risk the attrition of human existence. In a way, it is even more simple than that: It is just essential to become and to be poor.[13]

Without using our terminology, Stringfellow powerfully presents a contemporary and relevant way of disengaging oneself from his own structure of security, while at the same time taking the structures seriously for what they make of others' lives.

At the same time, we are far from suggesting that the claim of Christian action is a claim for heroic individualism. Obedience and thanksgiving to God, not heroic self-expression, are the key. And the outward form and degree of freedom from conventional patterns will vary. Here Protestants have much to learn from Catholics, for the Catholic tradition provides a wide variety of expression of vocation in freedom from the

[13] William Stringfellow, *My People Is the Enemy* (New York: Holt, Rinehart and Winston, 1964), p. 44.

pattern of secular society. That these religious (monastic) patterns of vocation have in them their own rigidities should not blind Protestant eyes to the need for developing meaningful patterns of freedom from and within modern secular life. Woolman was able to intensify an existing pattern, that of the Friends' ministry, to make it the vehicle of his particular vocation. The contemporary Protestant who is groping to find a pattern of freedom from convention finds little guidance. Of course it is also true that no established pattern can solve the problem for everybody; it is one important function of self-forgetting love to find its way into situations of flux and change, and to strive, however uncertainly, to meet their demands.

Finally, we do not suggest that the inner freedom of love is to be shown in any particular form of visible freedom from conformity. The point is that true openness to the other, an openness which includes not only an understanding of what it is like to be in his place, but also a putting of the energies of one's self at the service of the other, can only be effective as a freedom from one's self and one's own setting in life. The actual expression of freedom and love will always be most varied. In practice most men will not see the claim of love as something that uproots them from the usual patterns of life-work, family, etc., but will find moments, crises, when they are called upon by the situation to respond in freedom and love. The exemplary figure, who models the whole outward expression of his life around a striving for a new grasp and expression of God's will, will always be the exception. A particular evidence of the quality of Woolman's openness was his ability to enter deeply into the human meaning of the existence of a group toward which most of his contemporaries were closed. In our situation, there is often apt to be an added barrier of active conflict between the groups that need to understand one another, which will affect the outward pattern of what they do to and for one another, but will not change the fundamental aspects of openness which we see in our illustration. We focus on Woolman not to suggest that he prefigures an ideal pattern, but to say that the freedom from being what one is expected to be, and the ability to "live into" the situation of the other, are aspects of self-giving in all its various forms.

VII
A Case in Point

On that day many will say to me, "Lord, Lord, did we not prophesy in your name, and cast out demons in your name, and do many mighty works in your name?" And then will I declare to them, "I never knew you; depart from me, you evildoers." (Matt. 7:22-23.)

For in Christ Jesus neither circumcision nor uncircumcision is of any avail, but faith working through love. (Gal. 5:6.)

At several stages in the discussion there has been a deliberate mention of justice as the social manifestation of Christian love. Although justice would seem generally to rule out the "equivocal" and the arbitrary, justice is certainly not understood in the same way by all persons. We have seen how an element of paradox or ambiguity characterizes every application or expression of Christian faith. We have also seen that the "application" is equally inevitable, that there is no Christian stance of inaction, no inactive Christian faith. To put the thesis to the test, let us examine one of the most important ethical issues facing contemporary man. Although the issues of sex, alienation, automation, war, population explosion, and Church and State are becoming increasingly important, the issue of racial justice in the social order of America is already in sharp focus. This issue will serve as a case in point.

The first demand of Christ upon the Christian is that he love, not that he be just. The peculiar quality of Christian love is such, however, that justice is a social manifestation of this love.[1] The peculiar quality of existing in love does not pass unambiguously over into acts of love. Further, to exist in God's love is not to extinguish all selfishness and defensiveness in oneself. *Agape,* or the Christian form of love, is connected with *libido* and *eros* to the extent that there is always an appetitive, gregarious, and preferential element in human love. Man's love is never wholly self-less or altruistic.[2] The inclination of a person to give priority to that which he knows, sees, desires, and prefers requires the inclusion of justice in Christian ethics. It is through justice that "unknown" others are protected from the discriminatory effects of our preferences. Consequently, love allies itself with justice in order to preserve the possibility of particular preference *and*

[1] Reinhold Niebuhr: "I still believe that love may be the motive of social action but that justice must be the instrument of love in a world in which self-interest is bound to defy the canons of love on every level." Preface to 1956 edition of *An Interpretation of Christian Ethics* (New York: Meridian Books, 1956).

[2] The words *libido, philia, eros,* and *agape* often appear in discussions of love. These indicate separate qualities which are nevertheless related in mature love. To place the issue in the terms of the previous discussion, *libido* and *eros* function within an achievement orientation, *agape* within a transfigured achievement orientation. The peculiar quality of Christian love is *agape,* although *agape* does not eliminate or completely transform *eros* and *libido.*

the love of neighbor, whether we actually "prefer" (or like) him or not.

Justice appropriately becomes a form through which love expresses itself in order to protect the other person whom one does not know from the arbitrariness which may be involved in one's preference for the one he does know. Thus, one marries one woman, exclusively and permanently. This is an act of preferential love. One does not marry womanhood, nor does one marry this woman *for a time* with a view to marrying others *seriatim* later. On the contrary, the vow of marriage is maintained in purity only as one "keeps himself to her so long as they both shall live." The preference and exclusion are not simply incidental but necessary to the expression of love. Yet there is really no intention here of discriminating against any other person or of denying to any other person the possibility of marriage. The only denial to others is the possibility of marrying this woman.

One will readily see that the instance of marriage is invoked to suggest a way in which one's preferences of certain persons as friends or associates might be respected without doing injury to those not preferred. It would be a senseless and inaccurate grasp of the issue if one changed the command, "Thou shalt love," into "Thou shalt prefer all neighbors." Whatever ethical orientation one adopts must handle the question of one's particular self as he is as well as the question of universality, a relation to all people. It is one of the peculiar strengths of Christian ethics that it can contain a universal thrust without giving way to a nonhistorical eternal moral law, and, at the same time, contain a concrete and realistic understanding of an individual historical existence without becoming altogether relativistic.

A Case in Point

It is through the relationship of justice to love that Christian ethics is able to affirm the "preferences" of persons, whether in association, friendship, or marriage, and at the same time to affirm a relation to all persons in the human family. One does not cease to be a self in affirming other selves. On the contrary, one can only affirm others as persons in terms of the self-understanding, the "person" quality, of oneself.[3] Love manifest in justice prevents love manifest in preference from being unjust. Within marriage, therefore, two persons do not deny others, but through their particular and exclusive affection they affirm all persons inclusively as desiring acceptance, love, and sexual gratification. One can be realistic in affirming all persons, then, because he is realistic about himself. Justice makes this possible, while love makes it necessary.[4]

[3] "The love for my own self is inseparably connected with the love for any other being. . . . Genuine love is an expression of productiveness and implies care, respect, responsibility, and knowledge. . . . Love of one person implies love of man as such. . . . Love of man is not, as is frequently supposed, an abstraction coming after the love for a specific person, but it is its premise, although genetically it is acquired in loving specific individuals.

"From this it follows that my own self must be as much an object of my love as another person. The *affirmation of one's own life, happiness, growth, freedom is rooted in one's capacity to love,* i.e., in care, respect, responsibility, and knowledge. If an individual is able to love productively, he loves himself too; if he can love *only* others, he cannot love at all." Erich Fromm, *The Art of Loving* (New York: Harper & Row, 1956), pp. 59-60.

While we agree with Fromm that affirmation of others as persons depends upon and is inextricable from affirmation of oneself, there is still a qualitative difference between an *eros* orientation of affirming myself even at cost to others and an *agape* orientation of affirming another even at a cost to myself.

[4] One is reminded of the famous statement of Reinhold Niebuhr: "Man's capacity for justice makes democracy possible; but man's inclination to injustice makes democracy necessary." *The Children of Light and the Children of Darkness* (New York: Charles Scribner's Sons, 1944), Foreword, p. xi.

Assuming, then, that justice is the expression of love in the social order, what is the meaning of justice? Natural law thinking inclines toward defining justice as "freedom from arbitrary treatment" or as that which appears right to a man as man. Paul Tillich suggests that there are levels of justice: intrinsic justice—the claim each person makes on the basis of his power of being; distributive justice—giving to everything in proportion to what it deserves; and creative justice—giving to another that which is needed in his situation to make possible his fulfillment and the fulfillment of all persons involved in the situation.

Both the natural law and Tillich's definitions are valuable, but both rest upon some sort of philosophical or theological base. Justice for secular man means one thing; justice for religious (or Christian) man may mean quite another. From the standpoint of religion, that is *just* which promotes the fullness of freedom, dignity, opportunity, and responsibility for a community of people. A minimum of equality of consideration and opportunity for all is assured through law, but the law cannot enforce personal fulfillment. It is assumed that the conscience of the people will be formed by their religious or moral commitments, not by the state. The state insists on a minimum as a base, without attempting to define the higher reaches of that "more excellent way." The minimum base is a freedom from arbitrary treatment guaranteed to all. But the cultivation of this freedom, the use one makes of his talent and of his gain—these depend upon the individual, his voluntary associations, his free commitments. The law can protect one from abuse by others, but not from self-abuse, from destruction by others, but not from self-destruction.

Freedom is sought, then, not as an end in itself, but as a necessary base for human fulfillment.[5]

The Christian in the contemporary American social order is under two constraints: a political one which is applicable to all citizens as citizens, regardless of their religious commitment; and a religious one, which is applicable to the committed members of a religious community. The political restraint is supported by force and must be obeyed or a penalty paid. The religious restraint is one of persuasion, and it is accepted as binding only as long as a person chooses to understand himself within a religious community.

Let us assume that a person is a Christian in the United States and that he is seeking to act as a Christian in the realm of race relations. What is his duty as a Christian? There is no detailed blueprint to inform the Christian in his action, no "canned" answer he can apply, no precise solution that has been on ice waiting to be thawed out, heated, and used, like a TV dinner. But there are guides which assist him toward a particular action—his own awareness of the

[5] This kind of freedom involves political as well as personal-moral freedom. It is not impossible without political freedom, however, and it is not guaranteed with political freedom. Helmut Thielicke concluded his address to the German *Bundestag* on German Unity Day, June 17, 1962, with the following words: "Das ist die provokatorische Frage, mit der ich schliessen muss. Es gibt Stunden, in denen Forderungen nur als *Heraus*forderungen hörbar gemacht werden können. Heute ist eine solche Stunde. Darum sei im Angesichte der abgetrennten Brüder noch einmal der entscheidende Satz gesagt: Freiheit heisst nicht, dass wir tun können, was wir wollen, sondern Freiheit heisst, dass wir werden dürfen, was wir sollen." (That is the provocative question with which I must finish. There are times when demands can be heard only as challenges. Today is such a time. Let the decisive statement be spoken again, therefore, in the presence of our separated brothers: Freedom does not mean that we can do what we wish, but rather that we may become what we should.) *An die Deutschen* (Tübingen: Rainer Wunderlich Verlag, 1962), p. 23. Cf. also *A Christian in East Germany* by Johannes Hamel (London: SCM Press, 1960).

wants and fears of a human being, his knowledge of the meaning of justice, and his existence in Christ. These guides combine to produce a way of arriving at a decision which is neither remotely general nor uniquely particular, but which, as a group of "relevant considerations," will set one on the way toward action as a Christian while allowing full sway to the unpredictable, unique, and spontaneous aspects of a particular situation. What are some "middle-axioms" or "pertinent considerations" that are applicable in this case? [6]

CONSIDERATIONS PERTINENT TO THE QUESTION OF RACE RELATIONS

1. *The act of God by which a person is forgiven in Christ also incorporates him as a member into an intersexual, interracial, and international community.* This community is brought into being by the special act of God in Christ. It is not an extension of preferences of kind, of natural likes and dislikes. In Christ men are given existence with and for one another. God's act in Christ is not best understood, then, as the saving of individuals but as the creation of a new community which is nurtured and sustained by Christ as spirit, power, and Lord.

[6] Professor John Bennett has developed a concept of "middle-axioms," more recently called "common ground morality" or "cultural constants." We choose to speak of "relevant considerations" in order to come closer to the situation of the *Christian* man and the immanence of natural law (or common ground morality or cultural constants) in an actual historical event. In a general way we agree with John Bennett in seeking functions which are more specific about particular actions than the pervasive command, "Thou shalt love," and yet more general than "Thou shalt withdraw from Vietnam" or "Thou shalt strike." "Relevant considerations" are useful to bring one closer to a correct decision about his specific duty as a Christian man by rehearsing factors which any Christian man should take into account in confronting the same problem.

This is not to suggest that sexual or cultural differences are abolished. One does not cease to be a man or woman when he becomes a Christian. Nor does he cease to be a Caucasian or a Negro, a Japanese or an American. Yet a community is created in Christ in which these differences do not become barriers that block the expression of love. On the contrary, the differences become the elements that make for a more splendid and versatile community. If "like" joins with "like" there is a "collection," a bland uniformity, not a community. If "unlike" joins with "unlike" there is a crowd. If persons with likenesses and unlikenesses come together, there is the possibility of a community. It is the claim of the Bible that God's act in Exodus-Sinai and in Christ does create such a genuine community—an existence-for-one-another of persons of different sex, race, nationality, and ability.[7]

2. *The needs of one person or racial group may be assumed to be the needs of another person or racial group.* It is quite easy to look at averages or extremes in differences between races at one particular point in their history and to infer from this comparison that the races are not human to the same

[7] Martin Buber may be taken as an interpreter of the Old Testament, speaking of the *melek,* the divine activity, creativity, and leadership. "These words fit our view that YHVH as 'God of Israel' does not become the lord of a cultic order of faith, shut up within itself, but the Lord of an order of people, covering all spheres of life——that is to say, a *melek.* . . . The 'social' element in the apodictic laws is to be understood not as the task of bettering the living conditions of society, but as that of establishing a true people, the covenant partner of the *melek;* the tribes are as yet a people only by God's act and not by their own. . . . The *melek* YHVH does not want to rule a crowd, but a community." From "Holy Event," *Writings of Martin Buber,* ed. Will Herberg (Gloucester, Mass.: Peter Smith, 1958), pp. 167-68.

Paul's statement in Galatians is pertinent for the New Testament. "For as many of you as were baptized into Christ have put on Christ. There is neither Jew nor Greek, there is neither slave nor free, there is neither male nor female; for you are all one in Christ Jesus." (3:27-28.)

extent. Putnam has done this sort of thing in *Race and Reason*.[8] Such a criterion of humanness becomes extremely selective and arbitrary, however. The case Putnam makes is particularly vulnerable at two points. First, he must eliminate the arts as indicative of humanness or intelligence. In the second place, he must speak of racial averages, not variations within races, variations which are more extensive than differences in averages between races. The pervasive error in Putnam's view, however, is to define humanness in terms of average intellectual ability rather than in terms of responsibility, individuality, trust, creativity, love, and the like. In terms of justice in the social order, the safest guide to relations between persons of different races and cultures is to assume that underneath various differences in ability and preferences, persons of all races seek the same kind of human fulfillment in work, social position, personal dignity and acceptance, love, play, economic security, health, and opportunity.

It is customary in the South for defenders of white supremacy to say that the Negro is not yet civilized enough to know what to do with freedom, power, and prosperity. This observation is made to justify the continuation of a paternalistic, protective, and patronizing attitude and activity toward all Negroes.

On the other hand there is a growing opinion among the Negroes that the white man is uncivilized, using the social-economic-political power of his position to retain that position at whatever cost. It is not yet known what the Negro in the South and in the United States will do with power; he has

[8] Carleton Putnam, *Race and Reason* (Washington, D.C.: Public Affairs Press, 1961). For a more adequate view, see, among others, L. C. Dunn and Theodosius Dobzhansky, *Heredity, Race and Society* (rev. ed.; New York: New American Library, 1952).

not yet had it. But there is a chance that he will use it in the interest of human and humane justice. The white man, however, has to the moment demonstrated his inability to be thoroughly civil through his countless indecencies and disfranchisements against the Negro.

The tragedy of both these views is that the status of an entire racial group of people is fixed. Surely, within the limits of one racial group it would be a mistake to treat all persons of all ages and all stages of development as being fully mature. The freedoms and responsibilities of a single ten-year-old are quite different from those of a married twenty-four-year-old person. But both are persons, and responsible action toward the ten-year-old is oriented toward that person's proper assumption of adult freedoms and responsibilities as he becomes older. Within the white community as within the Negro community there are persons of more and less maturity. No racial group of people is uniformly mature or uniformly adolescent.

3. *Whatever differences of aptitude, achievement, standard of living, educational, social, political, and economic opportunities are found within a racial group and between racial groups are data to be taken into account not in the definition of love for fellowmen but in all decisions and actions in expression of love.* In every culture there is a criterion of "health" which establishes the range within which people are free to move about as they please. If one goes further than that, however, and suggests that those who are "unhealthy" because of social, physical, intellectual, or psychological reasons are also "nonhuman," i.e., fundamentally different from the healthy ones, he handles callously the mystery of human existence. There are many differences between and within cultural

groups. Love toward particular persons, however, is not dependent upon the peculiar situations these persons are in. Love is a primary form of orientation in the relation to one's fellowman. Love is formative in a basic and independent way, creating an orientation toward another out of itself alone. Love is oriented to the *personness* of the other, not to the peculiarity of his situation. In all expressions of love, it is essential to consider human differences in the absence, use, misuse, and abuse of power. But in the primary orientation of love toward another, the other's degree of achievement, morality, intelligence, and the like, are not factors; "Thou shalt love" is an embracing requirement within a relationship of man with man. The fact that the other may be a criminal, a subversive, a syphilitic, an imbecile, a homosexual, or, indeed, an autocrat, a compulsive egoist, a drab conformist, or "owner of the town"—the fact of the other's status in no way alters the basic quality of the relationship. These differences become factors only when we seek to express love concretely in ways appropriate to particular persons in their particular circumstances.

4. *The possibility of injustice is reduced as multilateral participation in discussion and decision is increased.* The best guarantee against an inordinate insistence upon what is good for one racial group at the expense of another is to seek and consider the opinion of persons of the other group.[9] No one racial group has enough wisdom to decide what is good for another. And no racial group is virtuous enough to be entrusted with power to make decisions for another. Changes in

[9] Although the particular reference here is to racial groups, one might substitute "cultural group" for "racial group" in each instance to make the application more comprehensive.

race relations are as consequential for one racial group as for the other. These changes are best brought about, therefore, as a result of thorough consideration of these consequences by both racial groups together.

5. *The primary quality of the Christian's ethical life is love, a power which creates community among quite different kinds of persons, and which affirms a person in terms of his unique "being," not in terms of his exchangeable "worth."* We obscure the priority of love and love's relationship to technical or quantitative measures of meaning if we identify love and community with average income, standard of living, number of unemployed, etc., or, on the other hand, if we assume that there is no connection between love and average wage or percentage of voters in a particular community. Marxian utopianism is correct in being concerned about economic and social imbalance, but quite incorrect in orienting a society completely toward "sensible," tangible, quantifiable ends. Christian utopianism is correct in being concerned about the non-quantifiable, transcendent quality of mystery in relation to which man lives out his life, but quite incorrect in assuming that awareness of this quality inevitably brings about justice and consideration in the horizontal affairs of human life.

While not intending to decry or derogate man's interest in improving the situation in which he lives, we must nevertheless emphasize that for the Christian (as well as for many others) the meaning and depth of human existence, man's existence in trust, affection, and community, are of primary concern. Thus, as difficult as it is to achieve, and as arbitrary as it may appear to be, the central thrust of Christian ethics is toward the creation of community in such a way as to include consideration of quantitative standards without defining community in terms of them.

Whether or not a standard of living is sustained is a factor to be considered, but only as a secondary issue. Whether the educational standard of our schools is raised or lowered is a factor to be considered, but this is secondary to love. Whether industry will continue to come to our locality or not is a factor to be considered, but not as of first importance. Whether the housing pattern in a large city is upset or not is a factor, but not the most important one. Whether an institutional church is split or strengthened is a factor to be considered, but, again, it is one of secondary importance. Whether there will be intermarriage between white and Negro is a factor to be considered, but this, too, is not of first importance. Consequences in any of these regards which might accrue from changes in the social order should be considered, but the choice to love is not determined by the answer to any of these secondary questions. How love is expressed may be influenced by these factors, but not the disposition of love itself. Love considers these factors but it defers to none of them nor to all of them together.

How simple our moral problems would be if these "considerations" or some set of divine commands or biblical principles could be applied to each situation in slide-rule or mathematical fashion! But this is not the case. And as valuable as the "considerations" (axioms) are in clarifying and directing one's thought toward concrete action, no particular action is as yet prescribed. The Christian is not to use the neighbor to serve the axioms, but to use the axioms to serve the neighbor.

Does one picket the polls, join a protest demonstration,

give time and money to voter registration, contribute toward bond for arrested demonstrators, support the NAACP, CORE, SNCC, or participate in new ways yet to be suggested? Is any one of these a Christian action or an action forbidden the Christian? We maintain here that no Christian can decide for another what specific thing he should do for racial justice. The one power and command that is binding upon all Christians is to love, and love is the only unequivocal Christian action. But love is hardly an action in the sense of uniform conduct of all Christians in a specific circumstance, although unified, corporate action is often possible. Thus one Christian may express love by picketing, another by trying to persuade businesses, schools, and churches to open their services to all persons on the basis of the same standards, another in a program of education for citizenship. There is no one way of seeking social justice for all racial and cultural groups that is Christian, but the Christian is called inescapably to concern and action in this cause.

Let us go further now and sketch out the pattern of activity of one person who as a Christian is attempting to show love for his neighbors, Negro and white. His action takes place on the two levels mentioned above—the political and the religious.

POLITICAL ACTION

On the political level the Christian uses his voice and influence to assure equal protection before the law for all persons, the extension of the ballot to all citizens who are qualified on the basis of an impartial standard, and the openness of public services and tax-supported activities to all persons equally. Actually the Christian does these things not particularly because he is a Christian but because he is a citizen of the United States. Thus, any thoughtful citizen of whatever religious persuasion will be involved in some way in these activities. The great American experiment depends upon the full implementation of these opportunities for all citizens. For this reason the action of the United States government in the use of federal marshals and army troops to make possible James Meredith's entrance into the University of Mississippi in 1963 and in enacting and enforcing a law on Civil Rights was as proper and legitimate an exercise of federal power as was the use of the armed forces in the calling of Russia's hand on the missiles and missile bases in Cuba in 1962.

Neither the nation as a whole nor the individual is fully aware of all dimensions of injustice at any one time. Fortunately, that extent of awareness is not required. It is enough that once we as a people are alert to an injustice, an arbitrary treatment, we will take steps to compensate the fault and prevent its recurrence. Although the outcome of federal legislation to ensure voting rights for all citizens is not yet clear, the case of the Negro American is now before the American people in an inescapable way. The American people have the power to do something about the problem and, thankfully to say, they *are* doing something about it. The Christian will work in whatever ways are possible to him for those ends not only because he is an American citizen along with non-Christians, but also because he is a Christian who loves his fellowmen, Negro and white. Quite apart from additional things which Christian love might prompt him to do, the

Christian works for a standard of social justice that as a minimum is a guarantee to all persons in his society.[10]

But the meaning of love involves the Christian in far more extensive action than the political. He knows well that many people go along with the "new way" for all racial groups not because they agree with it or like it, but because they are forced to by the power of the law and of the state. He also knows that much anti-Negro or white supremacy sentiment is supported by supposedly Christian people, and in far too many instances is patently or openly endorsed or encouraged by the churches. The responsibility which rests uniquely upon the Christian includes not only the maintenance of a minimum standard of respect for others in public activity but also the motivation and attitudes of people and the implementation of love in the various contacts he has with Negro and white colleagues in human existence.

The most obvious public place where attitudes and motiva-

[10] There is both a positive and negative side to the question of public action for social and economic justice. Although the negative is never as important as the positive, it is of sufficient importance to emphasize. Every citizen is under obligation to involve himself in some way in the effort to achieve justice for all citizens. But every citizen is also under obligation to respect another person in a decision for a course of action different from his own. It is very easy for one to condemn the persons who demonstrate at voting places, restaurants, hotels, swimming pools, just as it is easy for one to condemn a conscientious objector. The fact that one does not himself feel called to that particular position is no warrant to condemn those who do so act. The Christian, then, will not only act, but he will be extremely careful about how he speaks of those who act differently. Differences in judgment, in comprehension of an issue, and in courage, are seldom sharp enough to justify the too easy remark that another who acts differently is a Communist, a subversive, or one engaging in un-American activities. Indeed, it is un-American to presume one's guilt before he is proved innocent. Thus, while we are called to be vigilant as to the security of our nation, we are also called to exercise a healthy and flexible reserve in dealing with those with whom we do not agree.

213

tions are formed is the religious community. This is also the most obvious place where Christian responsibility for participation in the radical dimensions of love rests. The limitations of political action lead us to consider the Christian's responsibility on the religious level.

ACTION IN THE CHURCH

The church does not belong to men except as God's gift and as man's activity in response to God's presence. It is patently presumptuous, therefore, for ushers and so-called "welcoming committees" to bar the entrance of any racial group to services of worship in a Christian church, as if the church belonged to men. It is incredible that Negroes are refused admission to "white" churches. Indeed, that one may even speak of "Negro" or "white" churches illustrates the fact that the white Christian and the Negro Christian have formulated their attitudes toward one another from a distance, in relative isolation. The community embracing Negro and white as well as bond and free, Greek and Jew, male and female, the unity of the Body of Christ, has been truncated and thwarted among Protestant and Roman Catholic churches in spite of the fact that in many of these churches the congregation regularly affirms belief in the Holy Catholic Church. Nowhere in society is the pathos of the present situation felt more painfully by the sensitive Christian than in the church, where racialism is allowed to fracture the unity of the Body of Christ.

The first work of the Christian toward social justice for all is to affirm the nature of God's work in Christ in the creation of the community called the church. He cannot rightfully move beyond the church to correct matters elsewhere until he has extended himself toward the opening of the church to all who come to worship, repent, adore, or pray. Opening the church involves the *inclusion* of a person in a community, not just allowing one to attend a meeting. Much of the discussion about race and religion has been on the relatively superficial level of deciding whether a Negro would be allowed to worship together with white persons, or white with Negro, in a regular service of worship. The substance of the issue is at the deeper level of the acknowledgment of the act of God's judgment and grace in Jesus Christ, an act which penetrates the superficial issue of who will be allowed to assemble in a particular place, and which accomplishes the work of creating an authentic community into which persons with many differences, including the racial, are initiated through baptism or confirmation. Our loss of the substance of the life of Christ's Holy Church is obvious in our speaking of "going to church" as if the church were a "place" to go, an activity to attend, a club to join. One may "go to Europe," or "go to Kiwanis," or "go to the opera," but one does not "go to church." The church is a community in Jesus Christ within which one lives. One is reborn not according to the will of his gregarious self, but according to the grace of God's Word. One may experience a new birth into a community of forgiveness and trust and henceforth live within the church, but he does not "go to it."

To become a member of Christ's church is to entrust oneself to the Christly Word of God. One is enabled to accept his life as God's gift to him, his former "achievement" orientation being transfigured.[11] He lives subsequently not in suspicion, envy, or fear, but in trust. One may live within a community of trust, but one does not "go to trust."

[11] See chap. IV.

Again, to become a member of Christ's church is to participate consciously and explicitly in the love of God for the
world and all people in it. Several dimensions of this peculiar
kind of Christian love have been emphasized in the preceding
pages. Love is no more an option for the Christian than is
faith. Love is the power and quality and substance of God's
activity toward us. To accept it is to live within it. To love is
to be changed in one's whole being—changed in attitude
toward others, changed in that upon which one's being feeds,
changed in that for which one hopes. Paul has written about
this change with bold clarity. "From now on, therefore, we
regard no one from a human point of view; even though we
once regarded Christ from a human point of view, we regard
him thus no longer. Therefore, if any one is in Christ, he is
a new creation; the old has passed away, behold, the new has
come." (II Cor. 5:16-17.) Love is a quality within which one
lives, that upon which he lives, and that which he expresses
in all his actions toward others; but one does not "go to love."

The first explicit work of the Christian, then, is to recover
within the church the powers of life, trust, and love which
give daily content to one's becoming a Christian and a member
of Christ's church. Once this is done, the Christian will affirm
in associations, business activities, casual contacts, common
meals, and civic projects, his respect and appreciation for the
Negro or white person as a neighbor, a fellowman, and, where
applicable, a fellow-Christian. Various kinds of opportunities
will fall to Christians of all ages for different acts of friendship. The world of daily activity is the "place" where Christian
faith is lived out, not in those activities which we usually
designate as "religious." Such "religious" activities as worship, attending Church School, doing considerate things to

others, supporting the church, etc., are, to be sure, legitimate acts of acknowledgment of the faith by which one lives. The real testing ground of faith, however, is not in any of these "religious" activities but in the common world in which every man lives, a world and a culture and a humanity toward which God's unconditioned love has been expressed in Christ.

It has been suggested above (particularly in chapter I) that much of the criticism (and/or the rejection) of Christianity and the church today is prompted more by a sensitive search for an authentic basis for Christian faith and morality than by a rejection or a contempt for morality and faith. It is our impression based upon contacts with college students during the last few years that they are not of one mind about anything, certainly not about religion. Underneath a surface acceptance of religion are many types of motivation and many questions. Underneath a surface rejection of religion and morality, there are many differences and much misinformation. Without overstating the case, we want to claim an authentic and sincere interest in religion and morality among an impressive percentage of college students today. If these students have not yet been able to commit themselves to the Christian faith or to a particular morality, this should not blind the observer to the positive virtues of independence, inquiry, sincerity, criticism, and courage which motivates them to reject a "phony" religion which is pretentious but insipid, loud but unsure, institutional but not communal, dogmatic but not personal, busy but without peace, moral but brittle, righteous but self-righteous, orthodox but without compassion.

As magnificent as the purest heritage of Christian faith continues to be today, an unprejudiced observer would find considerable evidence to document the suspicions of the students. Perhaps the issue centers around the taking of the present world and culture seriously, and the interpretation of the meaning of Christian faith in a nonprovincial way—that is, in such a way that faith continues to be viable within the context of increasing degrees of social, intellectual, geographical, and economic liberation. Can one be honest in today's world and be a Christian also? The identification of Christianity with such things as "free enterprise," "total abstinence," a "prudish" morality, economic success, health, anti-intellectualism, a particular metaphysics, anti-communism, dogmatism, ideology, white supremacy, peace with or without justice, and the like, has certainly made it difficult for a person growing up in America to become a Christian with an understanding of his bondage to God's presence through Christ in history and to the present world which God continues to love. It is exactly at this point that the church's understanding of herself as a group of people doing "religious" things, rather than as a community of persons who have been given a new life by God's grace in Jesus Christ, is confusing to the serious inquirer. The insipidity and blandness of popular Christianity in America today deserves the criticism and hostility of persons who believe that God does not ask the sacrifice of sincerity and honesty of any man to become a Christian or a member of the church. On the contrary, New Testament faith is not possible without sincerity and honesty.

THE ACTION OF THE CHURCH
WITHIN THE WORLD

What does all this have to do with the issue at hand? Very much, indeed, and we now turn to the central point. In some strange way Christian people have come to think of themselves as "saved" but not as transformed by faith manifesting itself in love. We tend to understand ourselves in terms of an eternal future in heaven at the expense of making and spending ourselves on behalf of justice for our fellowmen in today's existence. The church today may sing "Holy, holy, holy, Lord God of Hosts: Heaven and earth are full of thy glory!" once without an immersion in the struggle for the rights, dignity, and responsibility of all men, but not twice or thrice. It is now known too well within the Christian faith that God's righteousness creates a servant people, God's love a community of reconciliation upon the earth, for a cultic evasion of responsibility to occur. No one can think today that the Christian life is some sort of exemption from love and justice for all men in the present world in favor of a heavenly bliss. Two things should be said, therefore, about the relevance of the Christian's obligation to take this present existence seriously. First, that the need of one's neighbor as he now is in the present world imposes a direct obligation upon the Christian, and, second, that the neighbor is the neighbor regardless of his situation or affiliation. The Christian may have turned from the world in his religious pilgrimage because he did not find wholeness or sanctity in the world on its own terms. Seeking a resolution to a gnawing question at the center of his life he looked beyond the "world," its structures and powers, for that upon which the world depended, that which might give meaning to the world and human life within it. The turning away from the world exposed him to a Holiness which itself was turned toward the world and active in *agape* love, compassion, and healing for the world. Dietrich Bonhoeffer has expressed man's pilgrimage more succinctly than any other twentieth-century theologian in the poem "Christians and Unbelievers," quoted above,[12] and in one of his letters from prison.

Later I discovered and am still discovering up to this very moment that it is only by living completely in this world that one learns to believe. One must abandon every attempt to make something of oneself, whether it be a saint, a converted sinner, a churchman (the priestly type, so-called!), a righteous man or an unrighteous one, a sick man or a healthy one. This is what I mean by worldliness—taking life in one's stride, with all its duties and problems, its successes and failures, its experiences and helplessness. It is in such a life that we throw ourselves utterly in the arms of God and participate in his sufferings in the world and watch with Christ in Gethsemane. That is faith, that is *metanoia,* and that is what makes a man and a Christian (cf. Jeremiah 45). How can success make us arrogant or failure lead us astray, when we participate in the sufferings of God by living in this world?[13]

If the Christian is to acknowledge God not in heaven where man is not, but on the earth, in the world, where man is; if he is to serve God not primarily in acts of worship or acknowledgment but in acts of obedience, loyalty, justice, and compassion ("suffering" as Bonhoeffer puts it) in the daily life of this world, it is equally important that God is to be served in the world *as God.* The affirmation of the world as God's creation, forgiving love as God's act, the suffering of Jesus as the suffering of God, cannot be made on the basis of a scientific, objective reading of the data. If God is to be acknowledged *as God,* this is done only in faith, the comprehensive mytho-poetic commitment of one's self to God as

<hr />

[12] P. 145.
[13] Bonhoeffer, Letter of July 21, 1944, written after he knew of the failure of the plot to assassinate Hitler on July 20.

God. The world of our present culture tends to obscure the operation of faith by emphasis upon man's responsibility for his own destiny and by an increasing use of technology and the machine. The qualitative juices of human life—trust, hope, forgiveness, healing, compassion—are quantified, weighed, and measured, and nonpersonal techniques are employed to trigger personal joy. All sorts of remedies are suggested under the label, "How to be happy though rejected," which in effect offer one the pleasures of human existence without his really having to be human, "Christianity without tears," as Huxley expressed it in *Brave New World*.

The *worldliness* of the Christian is an affirmation of the world and all persons in it because of the act of God in enfleshing his love for all men in Jesus Christ. According to the world's standards Jesus was a failure, a subversive against Judaism as a religion and against Rome as a state, one who deserved and received death. According to the faith of the Christian, it is Jesus in whom God himself is present with man in history, breaking the power of evil forces, bringing the powers of the kingdom of God whose ultimate victory is foreshadowed in the triumph of God even in the apparent "weakness" of Jesus. The Christian's full engagement in the human struggle in the world is an engagement within a religious awareness and a religious commitment. His relation to the world is dialectical. He denies the world as having its being in itself or as understood only by observable data, and he affirms the world as having its reality in God's creativity or as understood by a combination of the observable data and mytho-poetic religious faith.

Having accepted his responsibility in and for the world,

with no immunities, no special privileges, the Christian man claims justice for his neighbor in all the sordid and sublime dimensions of their common life. It is part of the peculiar quality of love that it is aggressive and active in claiming the rights of others. One of the most regrettable aspects of the racial crisis in America today is the passivity of a supposedly "Christian people." Surely the Negro as well as the white man sees that demonstrations and other ways of claiming justice are only second-best from the standpoint of faith, and that inordinate amounts of willfulness, aggressiveness, and moralization get mixed up with the effort to claim one's own rights. The peculiarly Christian quality in this issue is that one does not claim his own right, as love does not "seek its own," but that one seeks the rights of his neighbor.

A major responsibility for the present injustice lies upon the white Christian community for its failure to express the love of God in this world by claiming economic, political, and social justice for all one's neighbors, particularly for Negro Americans. No Christian should leave another to the necessity of claiming justice for himself. The vast gap between this norm and the actual practice of most of us points up the need for and the potentialities of the Negro revolution. Initiative for change will come increasingly from the Negro side, and American Negroes will not maintain the patience which they have so far shown.

The riots in Chicago and Los Angeles, in Philadelphia and Atlanta, and the shrill cry of "Black Power" pierce the complacency of those who work patiently for progress through law, striking terror in the hearts of most American people, black and white. What is one to make of this new form of action? What is its cause? How is one to respond to it?

Is it possible to condone it? Is it possible to understand it and not condone it?

Robert W. Spike has editorialized on the "riots as communication." [14] It is quite clear that there is a message to be communicated in the riots, a message which we, tragically, would fail to receive if we were content simply to quiet with force the threat to public order. Underneath the periodic explosions is an increasing sense of disappointment, frustration, envy, and despair: disappointment that hopes for new dignity and opportunity have gone unrealized and that perhaps there are really no allies in the white community; frustration that the various aspects of his life—employment, wages, education, housing, voting—seem to stay the same no matter what anyone does; envy that many succeed without regard to human worth, while they themselves are doomed to fail without regard to human worth; despair because no one seems really to see them, to hear them, to care about them. Add to this the general uncertainties of the war and the vague feeling modern man has that something can be done about every problem. The result is a heady and volatile mixture which is the stuff of irrational and formless flailings at whoever and whatever is at hand, as well as the stuff of courageous and sober action for a new kind of human life.

The intellectual orientation which sustains the explosions and provides a connection between them is the conviction that it is fruitless to work "within the framework of the liberal establishment and society's institutions as they now exist." [15] If no imaginable situation could be worse, and if changes

[14] *Christianity and Crisis,* Vol. XXVI, No. 15, September 19, 1966.
[15] Pat Watters, "Encounter With the Future," *New South,* Vol. XX, No. 5, May 1965, p. 21.

which the "liberal establishment" makes turn out not to be changes at all, it is understandable that many would resort to radical action. Pat Watters, staff writer for the Southern Regional Council, tells of a remark by a worker in the Freedom Movement: "The trouble with you is that you don't wake up every morning like I do, hating America." The bitterness was clear in the chanting and singing of those in the Meredith March in 1966. "Ho-ho, whatta you know. White folks gotta go." "I love everybody, I love everybody, I love everybody in my heart, I just told a lie, I just told a lie, I just told a lie in my heart." "Jingle bells, shotgun shells, Freedom all the way, Oh what fun it is to blast a trooper man away." [16]

Without going further into the question of Black Power, it is clear that the militancy of a part of the civil rights movement has, in effect, put in question the function of law in the United States and, as a consequence, has threatened the constituency of the franchised, putting a critical tension between the movement and the majority of the citizenry.

The presence of the radical wing of the civil rights movement, "shock minorities" as Jacques Maritain calls them,[17] forces us not only to assess the issue they raise but also to devise some way of relating to the shock group itself. We agree with Maritain that these minorities play a needed role in democratic society, a prophetic role. But there are true prophets and false prophets, the former evoking the freshest and most sensitive expressions of the humanness to which the community aspires, the latter appealing to the darker, clan-

---

[16] Reported by Paul Good in "The Meredith March," *New South,* Vol. XXI, No. 3, Summer, 1966, p. 3.

[17] In "The Democratic Manifesto" in *Man and the State* (Chicago: The University of Chicago Press, 1951).

destine instincts of hatred and destructiveness. A shock minority which serves the community by awakening it, by shaking a pattern which has become repressive, by imparting to the community a grasp of new possibilities for individual and corporate dignity of existence is a most constructive force and deserves the protection of law. On the other hand, a shock minority may feed on the plight of people, compounding their dilemma by manipulating them, by using them, by offering a solution that is worse than the problem, by tearing the fabric of the human community and thus destroying a possibility for all the persons involved. In this case, the shock minority is to be restrained by the community for the health of the minority and of the community generally.

What Christian faith has to do with this kind of question is not exactly clear. The traditional functions of encouraging the discipline needed for order and of urging both rehabilitation and forgiveness continue to be relevant. But Christian faith can go beyond that and influence the mood and tone of a situation of conflict. Rightly understood Christian faith can mean much for mutual openness, so that the claim for justice can be made frankly and without crippling resentment. At the same time, it can, for both groups, provide a perspective within which the members of each group can appreciate the fundamental humanness of all. Further, this very openness will be a reminder to all who are seriously engaged in this area, in their various positions, of the higher judgment under which their particular group-claims stand, thus purging them from the tendency to identify their own insights and opinions with the Will of God.

The second major implication of this point of view has to do with the relation between the Christian and the non-Christian in the world. Some persons will accept the position to this point, but will restrict the Christian's responsibility within the world to fellow Christians. They will emphasize the church as a community of reconciliation which is founded on God's love in Christ and which is transracial, transnational, and transsexual. But they draw a sharp line between the church as a fellowship of new men in Christ Jesus and persons who are not Christian. The Christian's responsibility for consideration and help as well as for justice to others is limited to those who qualify by being in the circle of the reborn.

Here again, however, the issue is clear, and the peculiar quality of Christian love is in jeopardy. It is true that Jesus admonished his hearers not to cast pearls before swine nor to give that which is holy to dogs (Matt. 7:6). Yet it would be a strained interpretation of this passage to use it to restrict the obligation of Christian charity to fellow Christians. Jesus' explicit teaching about love is to the contrary.

If you love those who love you, what credit is that to you? For even sinners love those who love them. And if you do good to those who do good to you, what credit is that to you? For even sinners do the same. And if you lend to those from whom you hope to receive, what credit is that to you? Even sinners lend to sinners, to receive as much again. But love your enemies, and do good, and lend, expecting nothing in return; and your reward will be great, and you will be sons of the Most High; for he is kind to the ungrateful and the selfish. Be merciful, even as your Father is merciful. (Luke 6:32-36.)

Paul's statement about love in I Corinthians 13 is against that interpretation also, as is his interpretation in Romans of the work of Christ as a death on our behalf while we were

226

still sinners. Indeed, the arresting truth in the life and death of Jesus is that he exposed himself to whatever men chose to do to him while he suffered for their healing and bespoke for them God's blessing in the midst of their orgy of hate, vindictiveness, and fear.

There are passages which support the thesis that Jesus understood his career in terms of the saving of Israel, of his own people. But there is no way to bend the words or deeds of Jesus to make them applicable only to the "saved" of the house of Israel. On the contrary, he comes to call the sinner, not the righteous, to repentance (Mark 2:17), to save the "lost" of the household of Israel (Matt. 15:24).

Whatever justice the Christian seeks for any fellowman (including one of another race) is sought because that person is a man, a human being, who has needs which the Christian can supply. Whether that person is a Christian is not a factor in the situation. That person's claim is upon the Christian because he is a man in need, and because the Christian loves him as a fellowman. The Christian responds to the claim neither with the calculating purpose of "winning him for the church" nor with the idea of a later reciprocal favor. He responds because it is the spontaneous activity of the new life that he has been given in Christ to respond. It is his new nature to feel the pain of his neighbor and to live out in that interpersonal situation the qualities of healing and comfort, of brotherhood and peace.

Is it possible to cooperate with non-Christians in the effort to gain justice for all persons? By all means; it is not only possible but necessary. Many persons who make no profession to be Christian work sacrificially and effectively for justice. It is much more important for the Christian to identify the kind of work God in Christ is doing among men and to be engaged in this kind of work than it is to put the label "Christ" or "Christian" upon the work. The Christian's honest acknowledgment of the source of love for him through the worship of the church is important. But it is more important to claim the rightness of a function than of a name, the rightness of love and its works than the identification of all love with Christ. Indeed, it is only possible to acknowledge that Jesus is Messiah or Lord if one sees him as the one whom God sent to "live out" God's love for the world.

The Christian eagerly joins all persons who seek justice for all men. He joins cause with them whether they are Christian or not. And he joins cause with them for persons in want, whether those persons are Christian or not.

At long last, is one able to say quite specifically what a Christian as a Christian should do in the church and in the social order to achieve brotherhood and justice? No, not in terms of specific actions binding on all. A non-Christian may perform the same specific action that the Christian performs. In neither case does the specific action make one a Christian. On the other hand, two sincere Christians may be involved in different specific actions. The difference in specific action does not mean that one or the other is not a Christian.

There is, however, a peculiar style of life which is characteristic of all Christians, a style of withdrawal and return, of abandon and intense involvement, of radical moral sensitivity and vigor, of dispassionate consideration of the facts and a spontaneous venturing beyond the "facts," of denial and affirmation, of worship and work. In this particular issue of justice, we suggested several relevant considerations that would characterize a Christian's approach to the problem, but these do not prescribe a set pattern of specific acts. The mystery of Christian vocation and the nature of faith make impossible the designation of specific acts as "Christian." But that action of an individual person who through acceptance of God's grace in Jesus Christ has been turned from the desire to be righteous to the sincere love of his neighbor is *for him a Christian action.* He has broad freedom to act as pleases him, because no act of his can be ultimately wrong in the sense of separating him from the love of God. Yet at the same time he is given a narrow way, because he seeks the welfare, health, and full humanness of his neighbor. His neighbor's need is a claim upon him.

The life of the Christian is always dialectical, love being active in faith, and faith being active in love. Luther comprehended the life of the Christian when he said that the Christian is the most free lord of all, subject to none; and the Christian is the most dutiful servant of all, subject to every man.[18] It is impossible to reduce the bondage to the freedom, the freedom to the bondage. They occur together, and the fully orbed life of the Christian will hold them together. For it is by bondage to Christ that one is made free to love one's neighbor, and it is in the bondage to Christ that one is made a servant to all. The Christian must act according to his best judgment as to what is most likely to establish justice for all races of people. This he is *free* to do because no wrong action can separate him from the love of God. This he is *obligated* to do because the joy of his neighbor has become his own. What this action is that becomes for him a "Christian action,"

---

[18] *A Treatise on Christian Liberty,* trans. of *Von der Freiheit eines Christenmenschen,* in *Works of Martin Luther* (The Philadelphia Edition [Philadelphia: Muhlenberg Press, 1943]), II, 312-48.

he cannot tell ahead of time. His orientation to God, to history, to his neighbor, and to himself is such, however, that he is open to the unique responses that may be elicited from him by the particular person in need in the human community.

The Christian must take a wide range of considerations into account. The facts of the case have their place. The possible effects of all courses of action must be considered. The relation of church and state in a particular instance must be realistically assessed. Certain particular means of expressing love and achieving justice are surely more promising than others in the long run. Yet the determinative issue for the Christian as he accepts responsibility for social, economic, and political justice is his own being, his participation in the Body of Christ through which the dialectical qualities of freedom and bondage, faith and love, are preserved. Christian action is informed by reason, tradition, and law, but the peculiar quality of Christian action is that it is action in faith, reason in the service of trust, tradition in the service of present openness, law in the service of the gospel.

VIII
Perplexed, but Not unto Despair

We are afflicted in every way, but not crushed; perplexed, but not driven to despair; persecuted, but not forsaken; struck down, but not destroyed. (II Cor. 4:8-9.)

See to it that no one makes a prey of you by philosophy and empty deceit, according to human tradition, according to the elemental spirits of the universe, and not according to Christ. For in him the whole fullness of deity dwells bodily, and you have come to fullness of life in him, who is the head of all rule and authority. (Col. 2:8-10.)

One of the insights which Kierkegaard and Bonhoeffer share is the recognition of the "incognito" of the Knight of Faith. There is no visible connection between the eternal and the temporal, no obviousness to the action of the Christian. This being the case, we must seek the identifying characteristic of Christian action in the inward orientation of that action, or in some combination of orientation and action. It is the purpose of this chapter to point out what is, in fact, peculiar to the ethical life of the Christian today, whether that happens to be visible and obvious or not.

Peculiarity is secondary in importance to adequacy, however, and we must also consider whether there is an adequate Christian ethic—that is, whether Christian morality has depth and continuity, breadth and flexibility. It is our conviction that in Christian faith there is an answer to the moral question on all four counts. As it happens, the answer to the question of adequacy is related to the question of peculiarity. And the answer to both questions within Christian faith is a "lived," not a "thought" or "possessed," answer, while, to be sure, thought and possessions are factors within the answer.

Herbert Butterfield concludes his book *Christianity and History* with these words:

Similarly Christianity is not tied to régimes—not compelled to regard the existing order as the very end of life and the embodiment of all our values. Christians have too often tried to put the brake on things in the past, but at the critical turning-points in history they have less reason than others to be afraid that a new kind of society or civilisation will leave them with nothing to live for. . . . I have nothing to say at the finish except that if one wants a permanent rock in life and goes deep enough for it, it is difficult for historical events to shake it. There are times when we can never meet the future with sufficient elasticity of mind, especially if we are locked in the contemporary systems of thought. We can do worse than remember a principle which both gives us a firm Rock and leaves us the maximum elasticity for our minds: the principle: Hold to Christ, and for the rest be totally uncommitted.[1]

[1] H. Butterfield, *Christianity and History* (New York: Charles Scribner's Sons, 1950), pp. 145-46.

In the course of the discussion up to this point we have sought to explain and to reject orthodox and humanistic alternatives which in one way or another sacrifice either firmness or flexibility, either the constructive or the critical dimensions of faith. Butterfield's statement claims a basis in Christian faith for both constructive firmness and critical flexibility. The intent of his statement is to establish a relationship between faith and history which will neither derive faith from factual history nor factual history from faith. Faith has to do with the single ultimate commitment of one's life, a commitment which is not likely to be shaken by fact-oriented history. This would suggest that there is something involved in "holding fast to Christ" which is beyond the capacity of the "facts" of history to confirm or deny but which, nevertheless, is relevant to and viable within the changing tide of events.

In this case, "holding fast to Christ" is more than holding fast to historic facts about Jesus. Indeed, our information about Jesus has increased during the last two hundred years, and our pattern of interpretation of his humanity has certainly been altered.[2] Nevertheless, the rock is still there. There is a relationship between facts of history, and "holding fast to Christ." But that relationship enables us to affirm and express faith *within* history; it does not allow us to derive faith *from* history. We have renounced all efforts within Christian faith, therefore, either to affirm human life without the ultimate dimension or to make out of God a kind of moral, institutional, or political lever against history. Doctrinaire or "code" approaches to the problem of human freedom and responsibility are as sterile as are dogmatic approaches to belief.

[2] Cf. the discussion in chap. II.

A Glimpse at the Landscape

At this point it is in order to recapitulate the case for a faith which affirms the transcendent without dogmatism, the historical without disjunctive atomism, the ethical without moralism, the creedal without literalism, the objective without objectivism, and the subjective without subjectivism. The overall position may be called a radical shift in orientation. The change in orientation has been expressed in several ways in the preceding chapters. If we keep in mind that a change in the paradigm within which one grasps an issue does not in itself completely nullify an alternative emphasis, we may reformulate the position of the book as follows.

1. *From revelation as a light thrown upon God to revelation as a light thrown by God upon the life of man.* It is customary to speak of revelation as God's manifestation or as God's self-manifestation. It is still quite proper to speak this way, but it is no longer possible to mean by such speech that God manifests himself in isolation from man's life, that history is transcended in a mystical identification of man with God, that God gives himself to be an object with distinct attributes such as omnipotence, omniscience, etc. The early Hebrew prescription against making graven images (Exod. 20:4) should have made it clear to us long ago that God is no more successfully objectified in concepts than in visual images. It makes little difference what God is like if he is in isolation. It makes much difference if God is understood contextually, if one accepts and understands his own life within the light God throws upon all the dimensions of man's situation in history.

2. *From the understanding of God's act as cosmological to a historical understanding of it.* Spatial concepts became pre-

dominant over temporal ones when, in the early centuries of the life of the Christian church, the radical eschatology of Jesus and the church gave way to Greek categories of interpretation. Even when temporal forms of expression were used, they were used "non-historically," as Tillich would say.[3] The effect of the spatialization of the understanding was to contain horizontal history and movement within a scheme of doctrine, a framework of eternal salvation, and a conception of the end of time. But history cannot be contained within an idea or a system. Hence, the life of Western man since 1500 may be understood as a series of assertions of man's historical consciousness against a political or religious idea which claimed to contain all movement within itself. In Bonhoeffer's picture of man "come of age," this liberation is complete. Time triumphs over space, history over thought. As Buber puts it, there is not the historization of the nonhistorical (the cosmological, in this instance),[4] but the affirmation of God's act in history, in the "center of the village" (Bonhoeffer), in the midst of man's temporally assertive existence. Contemporary man is not particularly interested in heaven, and neither is contemporary theology, unless heaven is relevant contextually to man's temporal life in the present.

3. *From a commission to man to have dominion over every living thing* (*Gen. 1:28, Ps. 8*) *to a calling to serve the needs of men* (*Isa. 49:6*). Although a proper exegesis of the passages dealing with God's commission to Adam and Eve and his commission to II Isaiah would be quite complicated, we use the passages to suggest a sharp difference between them;

[3] "Historical and Non-Historical Interpretation of History," an essay in *The Protestant Era* (Chicago: The University of Chicago Press, 1948).
[4] Martin Buber, "Holy Event," in *The Prophetic Faith* (New York: Harper & Row, 1960).

the first giving rise to a kind of religious imperialism, the second ruling out a Judeo-centric political world in favor of Israel's performing the function of a "servant" in order to achieve universal understanding. Paradoxically, the Christian story from Constantine through the Middle Ages reveals almost the reverse development; from the mission of Jesus to be a "ransom" for men (Mark 10:45) and the commission of Paul to the church to accept a ministry of reconciliation (II Cor. 5:18) to the military political conquest under the motto *in hoc signo vinces*. The mood of contemporary theological interpretation represents a recovery of the dimension of servanthood, of suffering, of participation in the suffering of God in the world. Hence, there is a rejection of political utopianism and a sober resumption of the stance of active witness and persuasion, of witness to the power of God in our midst. This stance eschews force in the expression of its witness because faith cannot be forced, because God's act of love in Christ can only be acknowledged in freedom. Further, the very witness itself is a form of service, for it represents a claim for the maturity and joy of another person within an act which brings to expression a community based on love and reconciliation. God calls man most basically and essentially not to conquer but to serve man to the glory of God.

4. *From an achievement orientation to a transfigured achievement orientation.* This idea is not easy to express, but the point is nonetheless significant. Man's obligation to act and to achieve is set within the gratuitous act of the Transcendent. The receiving of life, value, and being as a gift is the context within which the Christian understands and lives out his existence. The fact that all sorts of abuses and excuses are

made possible by one's claim that God is the initial and ultimate actor does not void the point. We have recognized that the action of God is related qualitatively, not quantitatively, to man's action, creating a situation in which man must act but in which his act cannot destroy the meaning of his own or anyone else's life. To be sure, such a recognition in no way excuses our acts of callousness and brutality, nor does it in any way go around the problem of pain and suffering. Man's full responsibility for action is accepted within the context of God's unconditional affirmation of man. The gospel is a word about God's grace, and the action of this word transfigures the self-centered achievement orientation of man by giving a value to man's life within which he may or may not succeed in achieving value. The gospel frees man from the necessity of achieving value for himself and enables him to turn toward his neighbor in a value-giving acceptance. This act toward one's neighbor is, in effect, a spontaneous and inevitable extension of the gift of value one receives from God.

5. *From historical heroism with a promise of eschatological fulfillment (the image of the Pilgrim) to historical courage within eschatological presence (the image of the Knight of Faith).* In both these positions there is a striking kind of courage, for neither contains a resentment against the present. However, in the Pilgrim image (for instance, in John Bunyan's *Pilgrim's Progress,* Pilgrim covers his ears to shut out the cries of his family) the emphasis is upon the heavenly city, or the future consummation. One manages his present relations with nature, parents, children, friends, and fellowmen in such a way as to gain the Holy City in the future. This suggests that God is not present in the ordinary relations of the present

world. In the Knight-of-Faith image the future-orientation is not lost, but the emphasis is upon the present, upon the powers of the Transcendent *within* present relations with nature, parents, children, friends, and fellowmen. Although the old age and the new age are radically different, they actually overlap in such a way that the Christian is called upon to act loyally toward the powers of the new age within the old. Hence, we are "afflicted in every way, but not crushed; perplexed, but not driven unto despair; persecuted, but not forsaken; struck down, but not destroyed."

6. *From men of correct action to men of authentic being.* There have been times in both Jewish and Christian history when being a Jew meant obeying the Law, doing the Jewish thing; when being a Christian meant obeying the teaching of Jesus or the code of the church, doing the Christian thing. Both these emphases became confusing in Christian history because the Law and the teaching of Jesus were made preceptual. This meant that they became isolated from the source of righteousness, the act of God celebrated in worship. It has been held in these pages, however, that authentic religious morality always unites teaching and deed, act of God and act of man, being and doing. Our contemporary cultural situation is such that we tend to overcompensate for the moral sterility of religion in the past century and to regard morality as religion. Although there is a pressing and undeniable timeliness in the moral emphasis, especially in the areas of war and race, and although the Christian will cooperate with other persons in all sorts of moral efforts, he will not allow himself to be drawn into identifying religious faith with morality. In spite of evidence in the present situation to the contrary, it is

really as important to recognize a distinction between faith and morality as it is to see the relationship between them. In saying that there is a shift of emphasis from doing to being, then, we are not rejecting action but insisting upon its locus in the "being" of personal life, in life that receives both the power and the substance of moral endeavor in an action of God that is acknowledged in worship.

7. From faith as world-transcending to faith as world-affirming. Although there is a close similarity here with 1. and 5. above, there is still a point to be made under the rubric of "faith and the world." Ebeling says that faith affirms the world as it was intended to be, as God's creation. Faith is activated, then, in the world, not as a world-denial but, dialectically, as denying the world as it thinks itself to be (autonomous, independent) while affirming the world as it really is, as God's creation. Robert McAfee Brown has recently written of one aspect of this kind of affirmation, referring to his move from Union Theological Seminary to Stanford University as one from "Jerusalem to Athens."

It is likely that I have not yet felt the full impact of this move; I still feel like an apprentice learning the tools of a new trade. But the move was undertaken out of a conviction that if the theological venture is really justified it must be able to sustain itself not only in the supportive atmosphere of a seminary community but also in the indifferent atmosphere of a secular university. This does not mean that devoted Christians are not to be found among the Stanford faculty and students, but these people constitute a small minority and for hours and even for days my contacts may be confined chiefly to those who are unconcerned about many of the things about which I care deeply.[5]

---

[5] *The Christian Century,* May 5, 1965, p. 577.

This does not mean that God's terms are imposed on the world, but that quite apart from what the world thinks, the Christian claims by faith to enact in his history God's valuation of the world, which is repeatedly affirmation. Should the Christian, then, resent the fact that the world laughs at God and seems to get by with it? Hardly! He may take joy in all real joy of man and suffer in all the sadness of man's misjudgment of joy. He may cry out in resentment against the crudeness and brutality of man's life, but he does not fall into hate or sulking. God's act of love affirms the world even in the world's folly. Acts of error and folly may fail, but love does not fail as long as it does not exchange itself for hard resentment of history or for envy. Benjamin Britten in the "War Requiem" incorporated a line of Wilfred Owen's to make the point.

> But they who love the greater love
> Lay down their life; they do not hate.[6]

8. *From the primacy of the individual to the primacy of the individual-communal.* Man comes to individual humanness through a nexus of relations with other people. As far as his processes of knowing and self-identification are concerned, he does not begin with individual selfhood and then posit or postulate the existence of other selves in a community. On the contrary, selfhood arises only within community. This may be taken as a psychological as well as a religious fact, indicating the primordial nature of the community both in terms of social life generally and in terms of the act of God which the

⁶ From "At a Calvary Near the Ancre," *The Poems of Wilfred Owen* (London: Chatto & Windus, 1931), p. 108.

Christian claims has founded the "body," the "community" within which he exists. Thus, there is a shift away from the idea of one's being created as an individual with an obligation to be kind to others, or to affiliate with others (imperative ethics), toward an understanding of one's self within a community in history (indicative ethics). Individuality is important, but it is secondary—both chronologically and logically. God's presence in Christ not only strengthens individuals to the point where they are able to form communities. Rather, God's presence itself creates a community of men. And it is really a *community* that God's presence creates, not a mere collective.

9. *From insular paternalism to open dialogue.* One of the heaviest burdens that God bears is what men who call themselves Christian have done in his name, particularly for the sake of the missionary enterprise or the statistical growth of the church. The question of the relation between the Christian and the non-Christian will receive further development below, but at the moment we should recognize the patronizing approach of Christians to persons outside the church (usually a particular church) or to persons of other religions as a veritable profanity against the name of Christ. There is much talk of protecting the uniqueness of Christianity in all relations with non-Christians. What can a Christian learn from a humanist or a Buddhist? one asks. And usually the answer is: "Nothing, except how barren life is outside of Christ." We have so misunderstood the Christ act that we actually think that we are carrying God's power and truth to other people. We think they are without God's presence if we do not go to them, that they are lost without our understanding of the

light, and that it would be a real accomplishment for God and for us if they could be converted to Christianity and become active members of the First Provincial Church of Christ. But, again, we may say with gratitude that there has been a shift toward appreciation and respect for the people of other cultures and religions. The attitude is no longer that we are right and they are wrong, but that God's work among us creates such a dimension of community that genuine dialogue is possible—dialogue between people(s) who are partially right and partially wrong.

The Nature of the Resolution

We may assume that the theoretical, metaphysical, and institutional resolutions of the human situation, emphases which have had their day in Christian history, are not viable options for contemporary man. The question for the Christian man today is: Without the benefit of an absolute system of thought, or an absolute book, or an absolute institution, what am I to think and do? How may I resolve the questions of faith and love, the present and the past, the present and the future?

The one thing that seems to be sure is that whatever resolution is open to man today must be a "lived resolution," a personal-moral-communal resolution. This means that the norms implicit in the "dated" resolutions are not sufficient and that man is forced to act toward a resolution without the kind of stability and assurance which once prevailed. He is exposed and naked in his situation to a considerable degree, without benefit of an unquestioned Christian thought or pattern of action or institutional affiliation. All men are not able to cope with this problem equally well, and, as a consequence,

242

man's most demonic as well as his most constructive, his most brutal as well as his most humane, possibilities come to expression in it. Confronted with the almost bestial morality of our days since 1935, we lose confidence in man and put strictures upon his freedom in order to control his abusive actions toward other people. In fear of man's possible or probable misuse of his powers, we move to reduce these powers by defining the area of their legitimate exercise too narrowly. The parent withholds freedom from the child far too long because the parent is waiting for the child to prove responsible enough for that freedom. The naïve dean in a college seeks to convince the students that they are free to make the decision that seems proper to them, giving them at the same time the benefit of his own recommendation. When the students decide against his recommendation, he informs them that they cannot act out their decision, that they were only free to make another decision. The protective church-school teacher is so eager to see that her Methodist students decide for total abstinence that she really grants them freedom only to make that decision.

In each of these instances, the fear of the misuse of freedom precluded the granting of freedom, and transformed the relationship between the community and the individual into a conditional one. The specific humanness of a person is recognized only when we take him to be an end in himself (Kant), a center of will and consciousness (Brightman), a "thou" (Buber). To surrender freedom because of its possible misuse is to pay too high a price for proper action.

At long last we must take a more explicit position in the face of two questions. What, if anything, does Christian faith add to ethics? What is the relation between the Christian and the non-Christian?

WHAT IS PECULIAR
ABOUT CHRISTIAN ETHICS?

If there is something characteristic or peculiar about the ethics of the Christian, and if that something cannot be defined as certain specific actions apart from faith and intention, or as a certain faith (as trust) and intention apart from actions, then we must look for that peculiar "something" in a combination of faith and action. Paul Lehmann speaks of this in terms of the *environment* of decision and of *parabolic* action.

For the Christian, the *environment* of decision, not the *rules* of decision, gives to behavior its ethical significance. . . . Consequently, Christian ethics in the tradition of the Reformation seeks to provide an analysis of the environment of decision in which the principal foundations and perceptual directives of behavior are displaced by *contextual foundations* and *parabolic directives*. In a word, *the environment of decision is the context for the ethical reality of conscience.*[7]

William Hamilton speaks of the "style of the Christian life." [8] Both Lehmann and Hamilton operate within the understanding that there is something particular about a "Christian" life, and they conceive this distinguishing characteristic as containing both stance and action. For the sake of simplicity we speak of the peculiarly Christian in terms of the "style" of the life of the Christian, of the church as a community of reconciliation, and of theological activity.

[7] Paul L. Lehmann, *Ethics in a Christian Context* (New York: Harper & Row, 1963), p. 347.
[8] William Hamilton, *The New Essence of Christianity* (New York: Association Press, 1961), pp. 119-59.

THE STYLE OF THE CHRISTIAN'S LIFE

There are many ways of characterizing the Christian, each likely to have some validity. In the thirteenth chapter of Paul's first letter to the Corinthians, the image of the Christian is that of a person of faith, hope, and love. In the preceding pages several suggestions have been made about the Christian's life, as that of standing at the edge of our possibility of awareness, or at the edge of our effort in ordinary things, as existing between the times, or as life in death, death in life (chapter II), as being enabled by God's love to be "there" for another person, as being strengthened to the point of granting freedom to another person (chapter III), as "authentic existence" (chapter IV), as a *quest for* the Holy and the fellowman within the *awareness of* the Holy and the fellowman (chapter IV), or as life in and for the humanness of man's life in the world (chapter V). Remembering these characteristics, let us emphasize the peculiarity of a Christian's morality by suggesting a "style of life," that of courage, suffering, and joy. These qualities are related (in a special way) to Paul's faith, hope, and love. Although there is a unique relation of courage to faith, joy to hope, and suffering to love, all three qualities function in faith, and in hope, and in love. One may speak of these, then, as characterizing the style of a Christian life, because each contains substance and flexibility; relation to past, present, and future; validity in terms of God's action without his becoming a *deus ex machina;* and validity in terms of man's action without a heroic achievement orientation.

The courage of the Christian man is impressive because it is neither compulsive nor conforming. In contrast with Aristotle, it is not the mean between cowardice and recklessness.

In contrast with Kant, it is not the acceptance of one's duty as a divine command. Christian courage is power decisively expressed to affirm the most positive possibility of humanness in a given situation. Courage may speak or not speak, act or not act, but always there is a sensitive assessing of the factors in the situation, a freedom both from traditional answers and from "differences for the sake of difference." The Christian man may therefore champion an unpopular cause, like admitting Red China to the United Nations, or work for renewed dimensions of patriotism, or against required prayer in the public schools, or for continued tax exemption of church property. His courage is founded on both horizontal and vertical forces, both historical predictability and openness to the new possibilities of every situation which God's presence creates.

The Christian is courageous because his own decision and action are essential to his own integrity as well as to his relations with other people, while at the same time his decision and action are made within the fabric of God's act in Christ to give human meaning to his life and the lives of others. From the standpoint of the other person the Christian *must* act, for he cares for another whom he has the power to assist. From the standpoint of God he *may* act, i.e., God's love for him whether he acts correctly or not creates the possibility of his acting not for his own salvation, and not in fear of losing his salvation, but for the sake of his fellowman. Perhaps the word "spontaneity" properly suggests the nature of Christian courage. Whatever is needful "at the moment," whether that is altogether unprecedented or has been done a thousand times, is what courage enables the Christian to do. Without knowing or being able to do *everything,* he knows and can do *something.* Courage is the moral side of faith. Faith as trusting God's acceptance of us in Christ creates the courage to act, even though that act may turn out to be harmful rather than helpful.

God is active in man's courageous action in two ways, then; to make man sensitive to God's work of fulfilling man's life through justice, mercy, consideration, and compassion, and to accept and affirm man (forgive him) in spite of his failure at these points. Thus the courage of the Christian is not limited to the sensational and heroic, but is in evidence whenever one expresses toward another the human and value-creating quality of God's presence, without appeals to external sanctions or to the "Christianness" of the act. The case for the act rests on its quality, its courage, not its Christianness. There are persons of courage who are not Christians. But there are no Christians, normatively speaking, who are not courageous.

The Christian also suffers. He suffers because he is not completely in control of his own existence and because he loves. He suffers, not in resigned acceptance of the incongruities of existence as did the writer of Ecclesiastes, but actively and deliberately, as a matter of decision. He does not exaggerate particular "evils" which he cannot understand, nor does he pretend to understand what he does not understand. Yet he decides for and within finiteness, for and within contingency, and for and within love. He decides for a life within the context of the life of God and the life of man.

Needless to say, we are not speaking of physical pain. Perhaps one should resign himself to physical pain, or seek medicinal sedation. Suffering for the Christian is an existential reality, suggested by torment or anguish, meaninglessness, fractions in relations of trust, acts of betrayal of loyalty,

247

alienation of affection, guilt. All these are structurally characteristic of "human existence." To choose against them is to refuse responsibility and to deny love. To resign oneself to them is to neutralize a dimension of human existence which is potent with religious meaning. To choose suffering is not to say no to life or to insist on suffering for itself. Suffering is chosen only because one decides for his fellowman and for the Living God.

It is true, however, that the choice of God and fellowman might increase suffering. To affirm God is to affirm a standard of transcendent action beyond what men might expect of one another. The question with which the prophets and Jesus confront one is: "What doth God require of thee?" And to love and affirm another person is to give him the dignity of freedom and responsibility and to participate (stand with him) in his use and misuse of these gifts. To acknowledge God is to be involved in God's claim upon us and upon our situation. To love another person is to be involved in the radical possibilities within his life for bestiality and for nobility.

Existentially speaking, no man can commit a "final" act, either logically or chronologically. The Christian knows this, and he suffers, because his present life is set within the warp and woof of God's action and his own, of concern for himself and concern for his neighbor, of success and failure, of actions which carry and those that miscarry, of the world as it chooses to be and the world as God wishes it to be, of the old age that is passing away and the new age that God is bringing. To accept one's place at the edge of human possibilities is to suffer the tragedy of a people made free by God's light but who nevertheless choose darkness instead of the light. God does not refuse a world that refuses him, and the Christian does not refuse a man who abuses him. The New Testament claim is that Jesus' suffering is to be understood as the way in which God is present in our world. It is thus that Paul can say in the first century that we are afflicted in every way but not crushed, treated as impostors, and yet are true; as unknown, and yet well known; as dying, and behold we live; as punished, and yet not killed. Bonhoeffer can say in the twentieth century that it is not some religious act which makes a Christian what he is, but participation in the suffering of God in the life of the world. There are persons who suffer who are not Christian. But there are no Christians, normatively speaking, who do not suffer.

A third dimension in the mix of the "life style" of the Christian is joy. It seems that suffering would rule out the quality of joy from the Christian life. But, paradoxically, it is in the most intense moments of existential pain that the power of God's presence gives rise to joy. In this case joy is not the opposite of sorrow or of suffering but the "yes-saying" to life within the combination of pleasure and pain made possible by the assurance that the powers of the future age are those which sustain, purify, and establish the present act of love. Hence, even in the presence of death or of tragedy, one is basically joyful, because the meaning of his life is fulfilled by love, not by success or continued existence.

It is easy to cheapen joy by identifying it with "happiness" or absence of pain. Christian joy, however, is always in context with courageous decision and suffering love. Joy suggests a quality of the being of a Christian, the set of his orientation in existence. It is the direct accompaniment of one's acceptance and living within God's "yes" to man in Jesus Christ. The good news, the gospel of the New Testament, consists not in announcing a life free of difficulty and suffering, but in the announcement of the presence of God to renew, to restore, to redeem the meaning of life within the polarities of pain and pleasure, of suffering and happiness. The joy of the Christian arises from his participation in the love of God in Christ. He knows with Paul that nothing can separate him from the love of God. He is free to accept responsibility, to act spontaneously, with the benefit of the deliberate care of the "relevant considerations" and the reflective power of reason. He trusts the love of God to heal the wrong and fragmentariness of his momentary act, sustaining the strength of the intention in the enrichment of continuing life.

The experience of God's grace becomes formative for the Christian's interpretation of the life of all men. Hence, by anticipation, by hope, he draws all existence into the future of God's action, imparting to all the love and the grace of the fragmentary experience, the reversal of the achievement orientation. The hope of the Christian is eschatological, not utopian. There are persons with real joy who are not Christians. But there are no Christians without joy.

Paul was able in I Corinthians 13 to say that love was greater than faith and hope. We are not able to say a similar thing about the parallel qualities, that now abide courage, suffering, and joy, and the greatest of these is suffering. The truth of the matter is that the choice of "style" as a way of designating the Christian life was deliberate, to indicate the interrelatedness of the qualities. One is not courageous at one time and hopeful at another time in sequence. Neither is one able to rank these qualities: one, two, three. They interpenetrate one another, although only one may seem to be present in a given situation. In terms of the case in point, the Christian acts courageously to claim the right of another, knowing that his action might in fact prejudice the case of the other, and knowing that this act is to some extent influenced by his own fear and ambition. He also suffers with and for those who are victimized by their situation. At the same time he is joyful, affirming the presence of God by acting in faith and suffering in love, confident that the final significance of this situation will be given by God in the freedom of his future. Conditions of oppression or abuse are challenges to both the privileged and the deprived, but in both cases one's situation as a Christian is that present meaning is possible in terms of courage, suffering, and hope.

The first and most significant contribution of Christian faith to ethics is the rejection of an insipid faith and an insensitive ethic by holding faith and ethics together in a style of life, a life of courage in suffering and hope, of suffering in courage and hope, and of hope in courage and suffering.

THE COMMUNITY OF RECONCILIATION

The church as a "communal form of reconciling power" is the context within which the conscience of the Christian is nurtured. To be sure, the life pattern of the Christian must be individually activated, but even in situations of spatial isolation the Christian is individualistic neither in his receiving of faith nor in his expression of faith. Faith gives meaning to individual persons, and this may be spoken of as healing, as revelation, or as salvation. But the meaning that is given is interpersonal, communal. Buber even says that revelation occurs between man and man to suggest revelation's negation of individualism.[9]

The church is a unique community in human history. Here all the dimensions of God's activity are enfleshed in a community, setting the life of the Christian within a corporate body in which God's gift of freedom is offered to a person and in which one may become increasingly sensitive to the actual needs of his neighbors. Here the particularly personal aspect of man's relation to God receives expression, for the unconditional love of God for man is specifically re-enacted by persons who are persuaded that this is the life for them. Here man really becomes free because he is liberated from the tyranny of the transcendent. He is offered freedom by God's grace, not by God's possession or creation of him. Possession is an improper term for interpersonal community. Here one becomes free from the creator by being freed from necessity. It is God's pleasure to create man *in* freedom and *for* freedom. Man is existentially related to God through freedom, not through necessity, a point that Bonhoeffer dwells upon in the *Letters and Papers from Prison*. It is one thing to make this claim verbally, it is another thing to mediate this freedom to another, actually to give freedom to another person. One person may do this for one other person, but the range of meaning of freedom is more tangibly suggested when a com-

[9] In the foreword to the collection of five essays for the English-speaking world under the title, *Between Man and Man,* Buber writes: "This course shows, in the unfolding of the question about the essence of man, that it is by beginning neither with the individual nor with the collectivity, but only with the reality of the mutual relation between man and man, that this essence can be grasped." Trans. by R. G. Smith (Fontana ed.; New York: Collins, 1961), p. 15.

munity of people of different abilities and habits, races and desires, incarnates and transmits the gift of freedom to a person.

Here in the church a man also becomes sensitive to and aware of the ambiguities, the hurts, and the privations within which many men live. Here there is uninhibited and unprejudiced clarification of what one who is forgiven by God may do in a world that is not the kingdom of God. Here there is a celebration of God's act of unconditional acceptance in such a way that the conscience is created and informed, but nonlegalistically. Here the paradoxical realities of forgiveness and moral obligation are held together in the only way possible, in an actual human community. These qualities which appear to exclude one another cannot be held together logically or quantitatively. In the church, however, the effect of the presence of the powers of man and of God, of the future and the present, of the horizontal and the transcendent, is to sustain both sides of Luther's strange statement that man is simultaneously a sinner (*peccator*) and forgiven (*iustus*). The community of reconciliation creates an environment in which one is totally forgiven and totally obligated, with the forgiveness not compromising the moral demand and the moral demand not compromising the forgiveness. It is precisely at this point that the qualitative uniqueness of the life of the church lies. The church is a paradoxical community, just as Jesus Christ is paradoxical and the life of the individual Christian is paradoxical. The church lives two kinds of truth, the truth of ultimacy, God's act in Christ, and the truth of the preliminary, what man ought to do and be day by day in horizontal affairs.

Granted that churches in many instances have not enfleshed these qualities, the true church continues to incarnate them. Many criticisms of the church fail to comprehend this paradoxical relation between forgiveness and morality. Alexander Miller tells of a letter he received from a friend. The friend heard that Miller was writing an essay on justification by faith alone. He wrote to warn Miller about the project, suggesting that justification by faith alone (forgiveness of sin) was the most effective scapegoat from moral responsibility man had ever devised.[10] Albert Camus' attack upon Christian faith is much more profound and cathartic, but, in the end, it also rests upon a misreading of the relation between freedom and responsibility, between the act of God and the act of man, between the grace of God and the moral responsibility of man.

Camus' warfare is against the tyranny of the gods, the offering of an answer, a "cure," without one's having really faced the question. The act of God does not give a horizontal "cure" or provide a horizontal answer. It is paradoxically related to man's efforts and responsibilities, accentuating the moral demand but creating the framework within which man acts in responsibility, a framework of acceptance "in spite of" moral failure. But the real difference between Camus and the Christian in the church is that life in the church is communal and supportive, not, as Camus thought, to the softening of responsibility or the reduction of the absurd, but to the placing of the absurd within a context of "gift" or "love" which is not absurd. That is, one may be honest about absurdity as well as about happiness and meaning. He is not

[10] Alexander Miller, *The Renewal of Man* (Garden City: Doubleday & Company, 1955), p. 81.

bound to the dogmatic, unparadoxical assertion that all is absurd or that nothing is absurd. He is freed from the necessity of either denying God or affirming him. This freedom is not "given" in such a way that one does not have to "activate" it, nor is it given against or in limitation of human creativity. The church lives grace *and* responsibility and, consequently, brings to historical expression both freedom of *being* and freedom of *action*. Camus must deny the freedom *to be* in order to have freedom of *action*. "But at the moment I am well aware that that higher liberty, that freedom to *be,* which alone can serve as basis for a truth, does not exist." [11] The church mediates freedom of being to a person in order that he might have freedom of action.

The courage, suffering, and joy of a Christian life-style, paradoxical as they are in themselves, are sustained and nurtured by the church. Both the *being* and the conscience (*action*) of the Christian are historically created in the community of reconciliation. Hence, the courage, suffering, and hope do not stand over against present history, but within present history. They are the forms within which one *may* celebrate the way in which depth, the nature of the ultimate, God, is present in and to man's actual history.

THEOLOGICAL ACTIVITY

If rationalization is understood as the bending of history to illuminate ideas, then theologization may be defined as the bending of ideas to illuminate history. In the mood of Buber and Ebeling, theology serves the Word of God by enabling

[11] Albert Camus, *The Myth of Sisyphus and Other Essays* (New York: Knopf, 1955), p. 42.

man to participate in the sphere of God's act in time and history with the peculiarly human function of decision in responsible freedom. The Christian theologian knows that the human is the sphere of the possible, not the necessary, and that God becomes relevant at that point in history at which man moves out of the womb in which God and certain actions of man *are necessary* and into the fascinating and threatening sphere of historical existence where God and certain actions of man *are possible*. The function of theology is to use every intellectual tool to prod man out of cosmic necessity into historical possibility, to make man historical.

This is a brash thing for the theologian to do. The task is tolerable for him only because he believes that nothing can separate him from the love of God, and because he has tasted the delights of history, the love of God being present in the delights. The theological activity of the Christian (an aspect of the vocation of every Christian) involves assisting in the birth of another into history and meaning. The particular meaning referred to is that of Paul, that we are "perplexed, but not driven to despair, . . . dying, and behold we live; as punished, and yet not killed; as sorrowful, yet always rejoicing; as poor, yet making many rich; as having nothing, and yet possessing everything." (II Cor. 4:8; 6:9-10.)

At one moment theological activity may open one toward vigorous action in the cause of education, health, dignity of human life, peace, or against poverty (cf. the "relevant considerations" in chapter VII). Indeed, he may seek to air-condition the desert. At other moments, theological activity may open one toward the mystery of God's coming to us, toward God's participation in our anguish and distress and his hallowing of our occasions with a "presence" too exquisite to tell.[12]

Throughout this essay we have used various figures of alternation. To some this may have suggested a sort of dualism which requires alternation to give each side its due. We have wanted to say, however, that the alternation is of another kind, that the Presence of God in man's history must be lived, that God's act and man's act are simultaneous. Living-the-Presence spills over our categories of conception and intention. The human cannot really contain the divine; hence, the movement, the activity, the alternation, the community. Man cannot comprehend God, but in the pattern of worship and work, withdrawal and return, passivity and activity, he can respond in richness and variety to the Beyond which comprehends man.

The Christian and the Non-Christian

The final question to be faced is one which has been just under the surface of much that has been said. What is the relation between the Christian and the non-Christian? Is the Christian the only authentic man? Here the answer is unequivocal. One does not have to be a Christian to be an authentic man, but being a Christian is one way of being an authentic man. Faith in Christ does not give the believer the proposition that Christianity is superior to all other religions or that all non-Christian ground is "sinking sand." These are theoretical judgments which may be thought and affirmed

[12] The Moments of Dominion
That happen on the Soul
And leave it with a Discontent
Too exquisite—to tell—

Emily Dickinson, "No. 627," *The Complete Poems of Emily Dickinson,* ed. Thomas H. Johnson (Boston: Little, Brown and Company, 1960), p. 309.

by Christian people, but no theoretical judgment belongs to the primary level of God's activity. Religious knowledge and truth are existential, not theoretical. Theoretical statements may be made by men of faith, but these are valid only as *for* or *against* other theoretical statements. Christian faith functions primarily as trust in God, not trust in the accuracy of theoretical statements. Yet, the act of trust is not unfocused, nor is it without theoretical or propositional implications. The obligation upon the Christian is to relate himself to persons outside the community of faith in such a way that the primary nature of faith as trusting God (which cannot be conceptualized) will be retained while certain conceptual or theoretical expressions arising out of this trust are given.

Trust in God means, for the Christian, the "living" of his existence within the Presence of God (Emmanuel, God with us!), a Presence which judges, creates, heals, renews, reconciles, and redeems. The effect of this trust is not to give answers about spatial questions, but to establish a center of value, meaning, and order in the stream of history, a center in which the man of faith consciously participates with the whole of his being. The God who is so trusted, the God of Jesus, the God acting in Jesus Christ, may be trusted because he loves man. Faith as trust is response to a gift, a gratuitous relationship into which it is not necessary for one to enter, but into which one *may* enter.

The relation of the Christian to the non-Christian is determined by the way the Christian has experienced God *and* by the nature of the God he has experienced. It is important that both these factors be operative in all action of "witnessing" and in all thought about "witnessing."

258

The God whom the Christian meets in Jesus as the Christ is ultimate in power and love, but the holiness of this God is focused for man in that kind of action which man refers to as gracious, merciful, compassionate, and creative. The grace of the God who is active in Jesus is called unconditional, therefore, to indicate what Paul calls being made righteous by God's gift, in spite of our goodness or evil. The transformation in man's relation to God which grace accomplishes is that man does not create God's grace, that man's every act is of the nature of response to God's act, and that God's grace operates "in spite of" man's acceptance or rejection of it, man's belief or disbelief in it, man's understanding of himself as a Buddhist, a humanist, or a Christian. Because the God of Jesus is love, because God loves man whether man loves him or not, one's non-Christianness does not qualify or change God's basic disposition toward him. Not even one's Buddhist, Moslem, or Jewish stance separates one from the love of God in Christ Jesus.

By removing the necessity of belief in Jesus as the Christ from the living of an authentic human life, God's act of unconditional love creates the possibility of man's historic action of decision in freedom. By removing the *necessity* of belief in him, God creates the real *possibility* of belief in him. Paradoxical as it may seem, then, it is the nature of the God the Christian experiences in Jesus as the Christ that orients the Christian in openness toward the non-Christian, liberating the non-Christian from particular dogmas and ideologies. The Christian's experience of *this God* frees him from the necessity of imposing his convictions on the non-Christian, and it creates for the non-Christian the actual *possibility* of belief in God by removing the *necessity* of belief.

The Christian witnesses in God's name to his neighbor by bringing God's nature to expression in the non-manipulative, freedom-bestowing relationship between them, by incarnating the strength of God's love through acts of justice and care. The God of love can only be acknowledged by one man before another man through love. Love is the soundness of the tree, and the tree is fruitful in many ways.

Equally important in "witnessing to Christ" is the way in which it is done. The manner of declaring one's faith obviously follows from the nature of that witnessed to. But what is obvious to one is not obvious to another. It is necessary to indicate, therefore, that one witnesses to Christ by respecting the "self" of the other person, his sense of honesty, *his* sense of what is appropriate and true *for him*. Regardless of how true the God of love is for the Christian, that God can be confessed by another only if God becomes, in truth, God to and for him. The task of the Christian is not to try to convince someone else that confession of Jesus as Lord will bring salvation or success, but to take seriously the self of the other person, to be a fellowman to another person, entering with him upon the human quest for meaning, love, and truth. In all instances, respect for honesty is a basic condition for communication and commitment. The non-Christian is thereby freed to be honest about what is true or untrue, painful or pleasant, authentic or inauthentic for him. The first act of any Christian's approach to another is to affirm the other's dignity, freedom of conscience, and honesty. Only upon this base of man-to-man community, of the truly human freedom-responsibility polarity, can the question of God arise. Only within this kind of relationship is it possible for that person or anyone else to accept or reject God's act in Christ.

The relation of the Christian to the non-Christian extends God's unconditional love by creating a situation for the non-Christian in which he can be honest. He may honestly believe in Christ; he may honestly not believe. Because the Christian knows that unbelief does not separate one from God, he operates on the basis of and encourages historical honesty. It is more important for the non-Christian to be honest than to believe. On the basis of honesty, there is the possibility of belief. While hoping that another might entrust himself to Christ, the man of Christian faith and love first creates the possibility of authentic faith for his neighbor. He continues to sustain the neighbor whatever the neighbor's decision about Christ may be.

And what may one hope for in this and all other situations? That everything will turn out well, that the world will become Christian, that one will live eternally, that God will be all in all, and that there will be perpetual peace? No, not really! The future is open, and the Christian possesses no propositional control of that openness. Man can only act in the present. The future act is God's. Yet man's present act is an act in hope. Man acts in hope when he honors God's act in the present by loving man (giving him freedom and responsibility) and by affirming God's love through acts of justice and mercy appropriate to the situation. The fruit of the action, the way of the future, the Christian properly recognizes as the work of God.

AFFIRMATION, NOT RESENTMENT

The Christian witnesses to his hope about the entire human situation by placing his present, limited, ambiguous act of love within the context of God's future. He does this without resentment or resignation, as a conscious and deliberate committing of life and action to the God whose grace he knows in Christ's suffering for all that is misguided, anxious, fragmentary, diseased, weak, or sinful. To ask more of God than this is to manifest distrust. For the authentic Christian it is enough to know that the final act belongs to him who, through Christ, loves all men and is present in man's history to sustain and comprehend the whole range of the creative works of man, to know that all of man's occasions may dance for joy. This is the firm rock with maximum elasticity of which Butterfield spoke.[13]

Worship is a characteristic activity of the Christian community. In every act of worship the firm rock and the radical elasticity are invoked as the community appropriates God's act in the past and future in such a way that persons are given freedom to act, to exist, to create, to think, to feel, and to love in the present. In the act of worship the Christian offers all the dimensions of his creative action to the glory of God, and he receives all the dimensions of God's creative action for the enriching of man's life. Rather than being the oppressive, legalistic, and restrictive relationship which some regard it to be, the authentic Christian claims the yoke of Christ to be a gift of human liberation and a call to lively and creative existence. The yoke involves being and action, love and justice, compassion and discrimination, loyalty and criticism, openness and conviction, success and failure, humiliation and exaltation, but it is a yoke within which he finds full freedom to be a man.

[13] See note 1 above.

Without being taken out of history with its threats and dilemmas, and without resorting to a technological or spiritual sedation of existence, the Christian community affirms this world by celebrating its vision of the Beyond in the midst of history—through courage, joy, and suffering, through faith, hope, and love. The Christian man does not resent history. On the contrary, he affirms history as the place of God's decisive action to break the dominion of "philosophy," of "empty deceit," of "human tradition," and of the "elemental spirits," thus opening to men the exciting possibility of action and passion, of intense fullness of life.

INDEX OF SCRIPTURE

(Numbers in italic indicate references to footnotes)

Index of Scripture

INDEX OF NAMES

(Numbers in italic indicate references to footnotes)

INDEX OF SUBJECTS